The Lutheran L

Book Three

Thanks for Leaving

Barb Froman Writing As

Kris Knorr

Morning West Publishing

Beavercreek OR

Morning West Publishing
Copyright 2014 Kris Knorr

Scripture taken from the Holy Bible, NIV. Copyright 1973, 1978, 1984 International Bible Society, Used by permission of Zondervan Bible Publishers

ISBN: 978-1-938-531-10-1

Other Books by Kris Knorr

Book One
Lutheran Ladies Circle: Plucking One String

Book Two
Lutheran Ladies Circle: Through The Knothole

In youth we learn; in age we understand.

—Marie Ebner-Eschenbach (1830-1916)
Austrian Writer

The Marble

T he purple marble rolled down the rubber-matted aisle. When the train crossed a rough intersection, it halted and jiggled on the black grooves in the runner. It was a regular marble. Nothing strange about it, except that it seemed to be on a trip like the people in the rail cars. It wasn't big like a Dozer marble. Just a pleasant purple orb with three air bubbles trapped inside from its birthing experience.

On a sharp curve outside of Deming, New Mexico, it hopped three grooves, ricocheted off the leg of a seat, and lodged between a pair of Keds. The sneakers had holes cut in the sides of the canvas, where sock- covered bunions peeked out. Had the old woman wearing the shoes not been sitting with her knees primly together, as the charm school matron had advised sixty-six years ago, she wouldn't have felt the marble *thunk* against her foot. She was following other people's advice more and more—which seemed strange because years ago, she'd rejected most everyone's "two-bit" counsel.

She picked up the marble, held it up to the fragile light of daybreak for a few seconds, and then pushed it into one of the pockets in her sweater. Finding something already there, she pulled out a tiny tin with a barely clad hula-girl on the front. She held out the metal box to the girl with weird spotted hair, sitting across from her. "Mint?"

The twenty-five-year-old's eyes snapped back to her magazine, embarrassed she'd been caught staring. Wearing a pretend smile, she shook her head. "No, thanks."

"Go ahead." The maraca rattle of mints sounded. "Don't worry. I'm not one of those tar-hags who'll talk your ear off until you hide in the baggage car to get away from me."

The young woman glanced up. Ocean-blue eyes stared at her. The grandmotherly face was framed by a white Dutch-boy hair-do. She knew why she had sat across from this old lady, even though her reserved seat was farther up the aisle. What was it about old people? They seemed to become more translucent and glowing the closer they came to the end of their lives.

Or maybe it was her own regrets darkening herself and making everything else look purer. Earlier, behind the ruse of her magazine, she'd secretly watched the old gal pat down her beige hundred-pocket sweater, take out a beret studded with pink rhinestones, clip it in her white hair, rub her cheeks, then turn to the window. The heavy rumble of train wheels seemed to click off time as the lined face stared, looking for something in the sunrise.

"You remind me of my Nana." The young woman lowered her magazine.

"I'm Aunt Ula." Her hand, furrowed with veins, held the mints higher, rattling them again.

An acquiescing smile crossed the young woman's face. Accepting the tin, she pushed the sliding lid open with her thumb.

"Don't take the pink ones. They're Tylenol."

The young woman's hand froze. Red oblong capsules chalked with mint dust mingled with white tablets in a pill salad.

"You remind me of Nana in more ways than one." She pushed the lid closed and held out the tin. "Are you traveling for business or pleasure?"

Aunt Ula had turned to the big windows. She didn't notice the proffered tin or the young woman's awkward refusal. Rays of light bladed a pink sky as the sun pushed into a new day.

"Neither." Her voice barely rose above the clack of the wheels. "I'm running away."

***

Old Houses

"Excuse me; did you say..."

Aunt Ula pinned the girl to her seat with a look. She could do that. After eighty-some years of practice, she could communicate whatever she wanted with her face. She could also burp and toot on command, though those skills weren't as useful as a good glare. Lately, she'd been using her talents on the neighbor's dog. Each time she stepped into the backyard, the mutt would snarl as though it would eat her if only it could get its schnozz through the chain links. It took two weeks of glowering, but she'd finally sent it scuttling to its hiding place under the porch. Heavens, but she could've used that stare when she was younger. Like wisdom, some things come too late.

The young woman across from her looked like she was about to bolt. Hands stiff on the armrests, skinny body tensed and tilted forward, eyes wide with concern and indecision. It would either be the conductor or Elder Services she called. Aunt Ula softened her expression and smiled. "Never mind, dear."

The twenty-five-year-old sat rigid and alert, scanning for clues and information. Aunt Ula shrugged, turning back to the flat, empty fields and barbed wire fences. She had her own graves to uproot on this trip; she didn't have the shovel-energy to dig through this girl's problems too. And Lord, it looked like she had 'em. Her white Marilyn Monroe dress had surely been painted on her body. The taut stitches in the bodice were pulled until a sneeze would blow out the seams. Scarlet roses circled the hem, matching the blood in her glass neck-amulet. Brown, round-toed cowboy boots adorned her feet. At one time, they'd

4

been expensive, inlaid with a red-leather word on each side: *Bang!* But now duct tape circled the ball of each foot, holding on the soles.

And that hair. What a muddle. A young mess—just like she had been at that age.

Aunt Ula heard the young woman lean back in her seat. The pounding push of the wheels filled the quiet gap between them. Outside, the sun, keeping to its October schedule, moved slowly, barely chasing away the gray of night. As they topped a small rise, Aunt Ula noticed a weathered, two-story house to the north.

Long-shadowed in daybreak, it stared back at her, alone on hard-scrabble acres. A gate slouched on one hinge where a cow had surely grazed in the field. A rope swing hung, unmoving, from a big-limbed maple, where—perhaps—a man had pushed a girl who thought she was in love. The long porch offered a place to watch the stars. Or a stage for a father to scream damnation when he discovered his daughter had left with the man.

The train car rushed past. Aunt Ula turned to stare at the darkness gaping from broken windows.

Old houses. They all reminded her of home.

Around them, a few people stretched and stirred, though there weren't many passengers. "I'm Matty." The young woman gave the mint tin back.

Aunt Ula settled it into a pocket. "So what are you doing on this train?"

"Returning to San Diego."

"Oh. That's where I'm going. But I didn't ask where you'd end up. I asked what you were *doing* here."

Matty cocked her head and squinted, scanning-for-information again.

"Sorry. One of the perks of being ancient is not pussyfooting with words. You can try it when you're young, but there's a heavy penalty. They usually wean it out of you by the time you reach middle age. So why're you riding the train? Seeing as how there's faster and cheaper ways to travel."

Indecision tinged the young woman's voice. "I went to New Mexico for a few days to clear my head."

"That what they call it now days? In my time we called it running away."

They stared at each other for several heartbeats until Matty put on a doesn't-matter-what-you-think face. "It's not running away, if you go back."

Aunt Ula smiled. The girl hadn't quite mastered the look. Her mouth had the right pucker, but her eyes still showed that she cared. She'd master the gaze someday. Unfortunately, it was heartbreak that honed the look.

"You said you were running away." Matty paused to let her words pick up weight. "Do *you* plan to go back?"

Aunt Ula focused on her lap, her legs still primly pressed together. "To...go...back," she said the words slowly as though each one carried an encyclopedia of information. Placing both hands on her knees, she fell silent.

"I'm sorry to get in your business. It's just that I left my Nana in a care facility back in Texas. I worry constantly about her. I'm sure someone must be worried about you." Matty touched the woman's arm.

"What?" Aunt Ula looked up. "Oh." She waved away the question. "I'm actually an old hand at taking off. This time I'm on the trail of a runaway girl."

"And you think she's on this train?"

"Oh. I *know* she is."

Somebody's Stayin'
Somebody's Goin' To War

T he two women sat in a small booth in the dining car. The white plates in front of them were sticky with the cinnamon glaze of sweet rolls. Matty watched Aunt Ula stir four packets of sugar into her hot tea.

"Really? You drink it like that?"

"No. I just do this to support Hawaii and help the cane industry."

Matty rolled her eyes and leaned back in the booth. "So tell me about the runaway."

Aunt Ula glanced out the window as though a starting place would appear on the barren rocks of "The Land of Enchantment." She blew away the steam over her cup, watching the tea tag waggle with the sway of the train. The smile of a memory crossed her lips. "It's a long story."

"It takes twenty hours to get to San Diego."

"All right. Perhaps you remember what it was like to be sixteen and three-quarters...."

It's always been challenging to be smart if you're a girl pushing the grown-up age of almost-seventeen. But years ago it was worse. Especially when there was a war going on and your father was a Lutheran pastor who was born a hundred years old, marched off the boat, and immediately missed Germany. He preached grace and forgiveness, but he practiced thunder and lightning. His family could listen to the radio, but that was it. No movies, dancing, or silly record players. The only approved suitors were farmer-boys, scrubbed pink and terrified of his bluster.

The young girl didn't pay much attention to the war, it was something happening overseas. A burr under her dad's cassock. He'd work anti-war messages into his sermons, grabbing the sides of the pulpit, leaning forward to eagle eye the congregation. "Many of us have family overseas, and that's why we solved Europe's problems once before during the Great War. But look how much good that did. If a man in this country cannot get a job to feed his family now, what business do we have getting mixed up in this European mess?"

He allowed the Ladies Circle to have Bingo-for-Britain nights. They sent cast-off clothing to English kids who got bombed out during the blitz, but it was unfathomable that his Fatherland was actually doing any of the injustices he'd heard on the radio. It must be politics. So, he banned the family from listening to the airwaves.

Then one Sunday, a parishioner called, saying, 'Hell had arrived.' The pastor turned on the radio, and the family gathered to listen. Pearl Harbor was in flames.

To a sixteen-year-old, it was terrible. They took all the dance music off the air. All they talked about for days and days was the war.

Most of the boys in town went away—just when she was old enough to date them. There was nothing left except old farmers and little kids—and *so* many women. She spent a lot of time at her friend's house. Patty's dad had enlisted right away. Patty's mother got a job. The girls listened to whatever they wanted on the radio and danced in the living room. They told each other, "If we can't see it from the front porch, who's to say it even exists?"

And then the girl's brother, Joe, got drafted. The pastor abhorred the thought of his son going to Germany to kill his grandparents, his cousins, and his neighbors living there.

Shouting matches filled the house about being a conscientious objector. Too bad. Joe insisted on doing his patriotic duty and joining his friends. When he left for boot camp, Pastor Haupt refused to hang the blue star in the window, showing that the household had someone serving. Mom Haupt put it up anyway. It was one of the few times she defied him.

One Sunday, a man in the Merchant Marine showed up at church. His height and wide shoulders made him hard to miss. It was also difficult to overlook his left hand when he removed his Captain's hat to talk to a lady. His thumb and forefinger tweezed the bill, but the other fingers were mutilated. Scarred, callused nubs. Reminders that this was a working man hauling ocean cargo wherever it was needed.

Then he'd nod at something a lady said and a lock of his hair would fall over one eye. The maimed hand was no longer noticeable. For three Sundays he was flooded with invitations for chicken dinners, not because he was the only eligible, intelligent, twenty-eight-year-old man for miles, but because he had real news of the fighting. And he told Pastor Haupt he'd convince him why a war was necessary.

The Captain traveled to Wichita and Tulsa, measuring odd-shaped parts coming out of plane plants. He sent instructions to his ship's carpenters for modifications to the cargo hold, but every spare minute, he returned to the Haupt house and had another go at the pastor.

"They were murdered," he shouted during one of their loud debates. "My brother, my friends, fellow Mariners. Torpedoed by German subs lying in wait off North Carolina's shoreline. Twenty ships in three months along the east coast, and war hadn't even been declared yet."

The pastor tried to say something, but the young man bulldozed over his words. "For the love of God." He banged the table. "They were transporting first aid and supplies to England." His face turned dark, his eyes smoldered. "And the U-boats didn't even pick up survivors. Not a soul lived."

He never did convince the pastor, but he convinced the sixteen-year-old. When he left to go back to his ship, she went with him—in the middle of the night.

"You were that girl, weren't you?" Matty asked.

"That was my first runaway. I got better at it as time went along."

Leopard Head

Several groups of people crowded the door of the dining car, waiting for a table and breakfast. Passing through them, the two women returned to their seats after a quick stop for morning necessities. Matty plopped in the seat directly across from Aunt Ula. "So did you make it to the state line before your father came after both of you with a shotgun?"

"Pshaw!" The old woman pulled a quilting hoop from the bag at her feet and unsnugged the needle from the fabric. "No one came looking for me."

"But you were only sixteen. How can a pastor let his daughter run away?"

Aunt Ula unkinked the thick blue thread, pulling the needle away from her quilt square. "Most girls in my town were married by sixteen. Why wait? Your beau may not come back from the war. It was considered a patriotic act—a reason for them to live through battle." Her head bent over her stitch, but her stare peered over the top of her glasses, straight at Matty. "But I doubt that was the reason the posse failed to follow."

"Your father—the pastor?"

"I was mad at him for so many years. A volcano of complaints. And now that I've seen about 25,000 more sunrises, I understand. Don't agree with him, but understand him. That doesn't seem fair, does it, that he charitably crosses my mind in my old age when he was so unkind to me in my youth?"

"I hate to poke my nose into your personal affairs." Matty rolled her glass amulet between her fingers, twirling the red liquid inside. "But I have a mom like your dad. From where I stand, your father gave up. He wasn't much of a parent."

"I used to think so too, dear." Aunt Ula pulled tight the stitch she'd taken. "But the truth is when I left, I hurt a whole bunch of people, not just him. It was *me* who abandoned my family."

"Matty's hand dropped the amulet and rubbed her neck, her eyes glazing with unshed tears. She tried to swallow, but her throat tightened around the sob rising from her gut. She got up and hurried down the aisle toward another car. Any car. Why had she sat there? Her seat was three rows up.

She stood in the door landing, wiping her snotty nose with the edge of her hand. Brown scrubby bushes and evenly spaced telephone poles zoomed past the porthole in the door. It was like a movie running too fast. It was like life. She knew why she'd sat there.

Her Nana was itty bitty and sharp-witted too. And she had that same look that skewered a person to their seat until she was done with them. At least she used to—before the stroke. Nana hadn't quite figured the truth of what was happening when they'd taken her to the senior's home.

"You're not going to leave me?" Matty could still feel the bony hands gripping her arm. "Your mother would, but you won't." Nana had looked at her mother and then her. Searching their faces. Looking for something. Just a small wisp would do.

Matty's mom pushed a ball of yarn and needles onto Nana's lap. "It's not bad here. You need nurses and handling. Now we gotta go. They'll take care of you. We'll visit."

Nana followed them, rolling her wheelchair, pleading all the way to the outer door, "Don't leave me. I don't want to stay."

"Don't look back," her mother ordered, gripping Matty's elbow and pulling her along. It won't make it easier."

But she had. Nana's hands still reached for them. Her mouth silently pleading, *Please. Please.* Her eyes still searching. Matty waved with a half-hearted smile, walking backward to watch her grandmother. That's when she saw the weathered, old face crumble into tears.

It brought her to a standstill whenever she saw it again in her mind. A soul abandoned. A face that had lost hope.

"You came back." Aunt Ula looked up from her work and smiled as Matty slid into the seat across from her.

"Uh...yeah." She fanned her cheeks. "I just needed to wash my face and freshen up."

"Well..." Aunt Ula paused mid-stitch, arching an eyebrow. "As you say, it isn't running away *if you come back.*" Matty turned away and swallowed.

Aunt Ula continued to look the gal over. Jiminy Crickets, but she was a puzzle of mismatched pieces. And I suppose, Lord, you want me to do something about it? You know this trip isn't about her? I'm on my own mission here. I'm not helping some Marilyn Monroe wanna-be who looks like part of her head is on fire. You can hand her off to some other yokel. Somebody more agreeable. I've waited a lifetime to make this trip.

Her thoughts zapped to a halt.

In Bible studies and sermons, people oozed about how God spoke to them, saying, "And then I heard the all-knowing voice of the Lord from somewhere inside, telling me what to do."

Phhhtt!! He had never talked to her. Seems He just stood around with His arms crossed, tapping His foot, and letting her rant until she heard how stupid she sounded. He was sneaky that way.

Okay. She'd cut her filibuster short. She'd help out. Maybe He'd even bless her trip and give her what she came for.

Her conscience stung her again. All right, all right. Striking a deal was out of the question. She'd tried—many times—only to discover there was no bargaining chip she could bring to the Creator of the Universe that He couldn't create for Himself.

She'd do it, but the Deity's choice to use an unwilling, old crank was irritating. And, Lord, *I'm not beating anybody over the head with a buncha Bible verses.*

She sighed as she stared at the leopard spots painted on the side of the young woman's scalp with a strip of orange hair on top. Matty seemed to have developed an intense interest in the fabric design of the seat next to her which was blue. Plain blue.

"So...that's an interesting hair-do. Think I could pull it off?" Aunt Ula frowned. "Did you go into a beauty shop and ask them to paint black and yellow targets on your head?"

Matty touched the peach-fuzz on the left side of her skull. "I had to shave the hair off first, and then paint the scalp. I keep shaving it back to a quarter-inch. Both sides were painted, but I let the right side grow out."

"And dyed the top red and orange. I especially like the way your spotted earrings match the leopard motif. Where're you from?"

"A tiny town in Texas. Clarksville."

"That's a unique style for a gal from Little Dixie. Are all the girls sportin' animals on their heads?"

"Oh, god no." Matty's laugh didn't reach her eyes. "I live in San Diego now. I did this for my mom. She loved to brush my hair. Never braided it. Or put it up in a twist. She just combed it like I was a long-hair cat. I was about six when she told me she wanted me to grow it out so she could cut it off and have a wig made for her. Boy, was she ticked when Nana whacked it short." Matty touched the bristly hairs over her leopard spots as she spoke. "My hair seemed to be the only part of me that Mom wanted." She turned her stare to the seat again.

The silence stretched between them, the pulse of the engine, the hum of the wheels buffering the rawness of her words.

It was times like these Aunt Ula felt useless. There were probably right words to say. Something that would comfort or take away ache. But most of her eighty-some years of experience had been filled with calling a jerk—a pain in the butt, and a sweetie-pie—a blessing. Diplomacy wasn't part of her vocabulary. What would a pastor say? Well, not her father. He wasn't a feely guy. He called strikes as he saw them.

Her thoughts kicked her when she saw her image reflected from the train window. Instead of her face, she saw her father's. Craphouse crickets! How had she even remotely turned out tactless like him—she hadn't been around him much.

"I'm not real good at this," Aunt Ula began, "but I'm sorry for your hurt. Your mother sounds like...well, she sounds like cross between a jack-ass and a witch."

"She is." Matty grabbed Aunt Ula's hand, nodding hard. "You have no idea."

"And that's why you live in San Diego and wear spots?"

Matty slouched back in her seat. "Yeah. I guess. Yeah."

High, scratchy laughter pieced the air as three women entered the car, returning from breakfast. The noise awakened two teens sleeping in their seats. They cast sour looks at the noisy ladies, pulled their blankets higher to their chins, and closed their eyes again.

The train hummed along the tracks. Sunbeams streamed through south-facing windows. A conductor worked his way along the aisle, pulling down shades in empty rows, offering to assist seated passengers if they wanted the light blocked.

Matty and Aunt Ula caught each other's eyes, the silence bouncing back and forth, waiting for the other one to speak.

"Soooo..." Matty let her Texas drawl surface. "What're *you* runnin' away from?"

Let It Ring

"Running away?" Aunt Ula asked. "You said it wasn't running away if you go back."

Matty pushed out of her duct-taped boots, using the toe of one foot against the heel of the other. "Okay. I'm listening."

"That's what I'm doing. This is my coming back trip."

"San Diego is your hometown?"

"No. Oklahoma. I'm going to a Lutheran Ladies Convention in San Diego. But I had to—"

"Are you going to answer that?"

"What?"

"Your phone has been buzzing." Matty pointed at the old woman's sweater as she nudged her boots beneath her seat.

"You sure?" Aunt Ula patted her sweater. "I didn't feel it." She pulled the phone from a bottom pocket, looked at the screen, and then stuffed it back into its woolen hiding place.

"It could be someone worried about you."

Aunt Ula swatted her suggestion back at her. "It was the woman I stole the phone from."

Matty's eyes popped wide. "You stole a phone?"

"It would've been pretty irresponsible to take off on a trip without being able to call for help, don'cha think? Although why I'm asking a leopard-head Texan beats me."

"It's ringing again."

"Why can't I feel the darn thing? I know it vibrates like a cheap washing machine." She wrestled her pocket to get the cell out and shoved it toward the young woman. "You talk to her. Speak like an English woman. Tell her you're going to the convention too, and we're having a jolly time, chatting it up."

Matty stared as if she'd been asked to mud wrestle naked. "No way! Man up and answer the phone."

"And to think, I almost let you use my magic hankie." Aunt Ula transferred her scowl from the young woman to the phone. Muttering, she studied the buttons and then answered with a laugh. "Haa. Haa. Ha. Wait a minute, girls. Let me see who's calling. Hello-o-o?" The last word slipped out like a sales clerk excited to meet her next customer.

"Where ARE you?" a frantic voice shouted.

"Kay!" Aunt Ula grinned into the phone, winking at the young woman. "It's Kay."

Matty could feel her eyebrows squinching together, trying to tie themselves into a knot. She pointed at the phone, mouthing, *Talk*.

"I caught the train just fine, Kay." Aunt Ula grinned. "Oh, we're having such a good time. Where are you?"

A voice vacillating between anger and concern carried over the cranked-up speaker. "We're where *you're* supposed to be. You took off to the convention by yourself? No explanation— just a note? That's crazy! What were you thinking?" And why did you take *my phone?* Why not Vera's?"

"Vera has a passcode on hers. Wasn't that smart of me? There are lots of people going to convention. That laughter you hear in the background is from three of my traveling companions. We're doing tequila shots." Aunt Ula held up the phone to catch the spurts of high, scratchy tittering coming from the women at the front of the car. "And I'm sitting with a most elegant, delightful friend. She catches leopards for a living."

"*Where* are you?"

"Oh, let me see. I'm not sure of the last town we passed." She looked out the window.

"Deming, New Mexico." Matty whispered.

"My British friend, Matty..." Aunt Ula hawk-eyed the young woman and mimed holding a cup of tea, her pinky extended.

"She says we're somewhere between Petticoat Junction and Paddington Station. Those English have such a wobbly sense of humor. It's all those kippers they eat, I guess."

Matty held up both palms, mouthing, *Are you kidding?*

Kay's electric-condensed voice came from the phone. "If there's a real person there, let me talk to her."

"Oh, you'll just love her." Aunt Ula pushed the phone into Matty's palm and ordered, "Be British." In a loud voice she announced, "This is Kay. She's an American and somewhat neurotic. Would you be a dear and assure her we're perfectly safe. There're no terrorists on the train."

Matty held the phone a moment, giving the old woman a question mark gaze. "Are you freakin' kidding me?" she whispered.

Aunt Ula held her hands up like a beggar, her face pinched, her mouth voicing a silent *Please. Please.*

A sharp stab of guilt tightened Matty's chest. People were worried about this woman. They needed to know she was safe. Why was this happening—to constantly be thrown into situations with old people?

Aunt Ula touched Matty's arm, whispering, "Please help."

Matty let out a sigh as she turned away from her woebegone seatmate. "This is Matilda," she said in her best imitation of Downton Abbey. "How may I be of help?"

"Oh! Hello." The pause that followed was pregnant with reworded thoughts. "Uh...I'm Kay McCabe. I apologize. I didn't think you were real. Aunt Ula is prone to exaggerate to get her way."

"It's quite all right."

"I'm here with Aunt Ula's niece and the women of our Ladies Circle. We're driving to the national convention in San Diego. Is it true? Are you going?"

"To the Lutheran Ladies Convention?" Matty glanced at Aunt Ula, who was nodding rapidly. "Why...yes. Yes, I'm going there too."

"Is she all right? We don't let her travel alone. She can be...well, we're worried."

"Oh quite right. All is tickety-boo. We were gammering on about church and state, Muslims and mushrooms. We were just having a lark about your pilfered phone. What a gobfot, hey?" Matty shrugged.

"That's a relief." The sound of Kay's fading anxiety carried over the miles. "Matilda...I hate to ask you this, but given the circumstances, I don't know who else to ask. Would you mind calling if there's a problem before we can meet the train? She can be somewhat eccentric."

"Are you expecting a problem? Does she take any meds?"

"Oh no. She's healthier than an astronaut. Just quirky."

"Well, we can all get a bit bee-smacked. I assure you, all is well here. And, yes, of course, I'll look out for her. It would be my...Samaritan duty." Matty turned toward the beaming face across from her, the soft skin at the corner of those eyes crinkling like Nana's with a smile. And how did old people smirch their mouths to one side to make that mischievous look? Her British accent faded away. "I'll need your phone number."

Aunt Ula wrestled the phone from Matty's hand, hissing, "Fine limey you are." Into the cell she announced, "Never mind, I've got your number here. You're cutting out. We're going into a tunnel."

A new voice thundered through the speaker. "What do you think you're doing?"

Aunt Ula's shoulders slouched as she shook her head, whispering to Matty, "Vera. My relative. She's as much fun as an IRS auditor."

Hello! Are you there? blared from the phone.

"Vera!" Aunt Ula shouted back. "I'm having such a great time without you."

"What would ever possess you to take off like this? You can't travel alone."

"I couldn't ride in that van for three days with Kitty. It would drive me nuts. She hijacks every conversation to talk about her damn dog."

There was silence, then fumbling sounds.

"You had me on speaker, didn't you?" Aunt Ula said into the phone. "Well, you can thank me later. None of you were willing to confront her about it."

"We're coming to pick you up," an angrier-sounding Vera blared through the phone. "Tell us where you are."

"Well, you'd better drive like Batman 'cause I'll be in San Diego soon. Meet ya there." Grinning, Aunt Ula punched the End Call button.

"They can track that phone, you know."

"Fix it." Aunt Ula tossed it onto Matty's lap. "Vera's such a rattlebug she'll catch a plane and be waiting at the next station if she knows where I am."

"Did you steal the charging cord too?" The old lady shook her head. "Well, that's the only reason I'm turning this off. To save the battery. And why did I have to use a British accent?"

Aunt Ula shrugged. "It sounds bossy. Vera would like that. She's a control nut."

"I thought you church women were...uh..."

"Holy? Sweet-tempered? Empty-headed? Prim? Church ladies get a bad rap."

"You ran away so you didn't have to ride across country with a woman obsessed with her dog?"

"No. That was a bonus." Aunt Ula picked up her quilt hoop again. The stitches she'd sewn across the fabric looked like drunk-chicken tracks. Without much thought, she plunged her needle into the material and pulled through another stitch.

20

"Vera is my only relative. She's really a cousin, but I make everyone call me Aunt Ula. It helps with the pecking order. Besides, I was the black stain on the Haupt family. It was forbidden to talk about me. She doesn't know my history. No one does. You heard them. They treat me like a child. Think I'm missing a few of my polka dots."

Matty cocked one eyebrow higher than the other.

"But I'm not. I'm collecting pieces of my past on this trip. I'm like a goose flying south or a salmon nosing back upstream. They don't know why they're doing it, but it's a need deeper than hunger. I ache to touch the places I've lived. I don't know what I'm supposed to get out of it. I only know it pulls at me constantly. I can't go forward until I've looked back at where I've been."

"So you're starting your search for your past in San Diego?"

"Oh no, dear." Aunt Ula checked the thin gold watch on her wrist. "It actually started over sixty years ago on this very train." She lifted a foot, wiggling a red-plaid Keds in the air. The large bump of a bunion bulged through the hole cut in the side. "Riding this train is the reason my feet look like this today."

Waiting For A Train

A slight breeze rolled in from the west. Stars watched from a cloudless sky. It had been thrilling. Like playing hide and seek at church camp after dark. Butterflies tingled in her stomach. She kept rubbing her midriff, trying to herd them into a corner behind a kidney. The man sitting next to her was beautiful. She didn't have to act dumb around him, or be accused of being a snobby preacher's kid. She'd gotten herself a man. A real man. She and her suitcase had sneaked out the back door at midnight and driven with him for two hours. It was exciting and romantic, just like the stories in *Women* magazine.

Until they arrived at the Oklahoma City Depot.

"C'mon." Captain Kolfred Kellner held out his hand, encouraging her out of the car. His voice was gentle, but Ula didn't move. Masses of people stood everywhere. There were so many lights; it was as bright as noontime. He rubbed her fingers gently between his. "Do you want to go home? I'll find someone to take you. I've *got* to be on this train."

In front of the Edsel, a woman in a dark blue dress had both arms wrapped around a man in an army uniform. She kissed him hard. Her large floppy hat fell off, but the woman didn't notice. Her lips stayed glued on the man.

"Ula? I *have* to get back to my ship. I've got supplies and a crew coming in. If you want to go home, I understand."

She looked at the snarl of people. What was worse? Hoping a stranger would take her home and not try to stop along the way or staying with the man she knew would protect her? She slid out of the car.

A green duffel hung from one shoulder of Kol's blue wool uniform. He used his body and her suitcase to nudge a path through the throng. They got separated once. The bile of panic rose in Ula's throat until she spotted his white Captain's hat. She grabbed a fistful of his jacket and pressed close, staying on his heels as he wormed though the crowd and got in a slow moving line.

It took a half hour for them to reach the front of the ticket window. The Captain used the time to chat and entertain a little boy while the mother went to the restroom. Ula felt him touch her chin. It wasn't until then she realized she'd been staring with her mouth open. So many people. A few women were crying. Many of the men laughed too loud. Cigarette smoke curled into the air, making a haze under the lights.

"Destination?" The man at the ticketing window yawned when they'd reached the front of the line.

Ula looked at the Captain. "Seattle." He slid documents and money through the cashier window. "Can you check if a cargo order got loaded in Wichita and which train it's on?"

"Not here. You're on Train 147. Car 4. Reserved seats 14 and 15. Leaves at 2:30." He pushed papers at them.

The Captain grabbed the tickets, and leaned close to Ula's ear, trying to speak over the rumble of voices as they walked away. "Do you want to wait in here or on the platform?"

The sharp squeal of a train whistle cut the air. Ula jumped, whipping her head around as though the locomotive might run through the lobby. "You'd think it was Armageddon," she called out.

The Captain put her suitcase against a column. "I need to check on cargo that's coming from Cessna. Stay right here, next to this pillar. Don't move, okay?" He patted her hand as he removed it from his gold-braided sleeve.

Her face paled. He took several steps, hesitated and turned around, his hand flared in a halt gesture. "Don't move. Stay right there. I'll be back."

His six-and-a-half feet of height allowed her to follow his hat through the crowd and out the doors. Her hand rubbed the hard plaster of the pillar, looking for something to grip. So this was war. There were public displays of affection all around her, couples kissing, an old man openly crying, holding onto a boy in dress khakis. Younger siblings had latched onto the boy's knees. The woman who must've been his mother pulled the kids away then pressed invisible wrinkles from his shoulders with her palm. She pushed a paper lunch sack into his hand then gave him a long look as though memorizing the face she'd given birth to. He grabbed her in a hug, his face pinched with unshed tears.

Ula looked away. This was the great tearing apart her father had ranted about. Panic squeezed her sixteen-year-old heart again. What if something happened to Kol and he couldn't get back to her? Hadn't she torn her own family apart by leaving? Wasn't that her just punishment—to be immediately ripped away from what she desired? She stood on her suitcase scanning the crowd. His captain's hat was nowhere in sight.

From a sign on the wall, a flyboy in a leather cap looked down on her with the message: *You buy 'em, we'll fly 'em. Defense Bond Stamps.* She thought he looked too chipper and happy—not at all like the families who were holding onto each other here. She stared at a picture of an empty plate instead. *Food is a Weapon. Don't Waste It. Buy It Wisely—Cook It Carefully—Eat It All.* She frowned. How stupid. Who didn't do that? But maybe that was because she was Lutheran. She wondered if Catholics and Episcopalians had to eat their plates clean too, or did they need to be ordered by the National Wartime Nutrition Program?

An announcement came over the loudspeakers, but it was garbled in the din of the constant noise. Kol wasn't in sight. A wave of people surged for the platform. It was past 2:30. She should have paid attention to which train they were on, but she'd been too busy making herself small and invisible. A throng pushed in from the parking lot, filling the gaps on the floor.

Her stomach tightened, pressing sour liquid up her throat. If she became stranded, how would she get home? Was she a married woman if she'd eloped, but he'd left her at the train station? Did her father have enough fuel stamps on his ration card? Would he even come?

"I hate war," she mumbled staring at the globed ceiling lights. She stood on her suitcase again. The only white hats in the room were Panamas, but she spotted the restrooms, next to the posters of pretty women: *VD. You Never Can Tell!*

Elbowing through the crowd, she made a trip to the bathroom, splashing water on her face to calm herself. Another scratchy announcement made women rush out the door. Ula joined the humming mass of bodies working their way to the platform. Kol was not in sight. She boggled at the lines of trains, not knowing which one she was supposed to be on or if it was there.

Leaning against a pole, she pressed her forehead to the cool metal. She'd disobeyed her father by running away. Disobeyed her husband by not staying where he'd put her. Stranded at a depot was the punishment she deserved. Maybe Kol would come back for her, but it wouldn't be soon. He had important cargo to sail to the east coast. If she could find a way home, no one but her family would know she'd ruined her reputation. She wouldn't even tell Patty.

The nearby train whistle blew, startling her into a wide-eyed jump. "And I hate trains," she groaned.

No Privacy In War

A man in a khaki uniform grabbed Ula under both arms, hefting her into the air. She screamed when he heaved her into the arms of another man in the throng. The next man grabbed her, one burly arm under her buttocks and one around her back, his hand brushing her bosom. Ula's eyes widened. She screamed again, swatting at the third pair of hands reaching for her.

"You're a little hell-cat." A red-haired private snugged her to his body.

Ula tried to kick, but the crowd pressed too close. The next pair of arms wrapped around her, trapping her hands, pressing her face into his chest. The man gave her a shake. "Stop it."

Ula squirmed, noticing for the first time she was standing on the steps of a train car. She looked up into Kol's eyes, then buried her face back into his chest, crying.

"Good luck with that 'un, Cap'n," a gruff voice shouted, followed by laughter from the crowd.

Kol waved, touching the brim of his hat. "Thanks for the assist, fellas." He let go of Ula to reach for her suitcase being passed through the crowd toward him.

"We've gotta clear the stairs," he said in Ula's ear, but she remained stiff, her face pressed into him. With one hand around her waist and the other around the suitcase, he hefted both up the steps into the luggage landing crowded with people.

"Stop it! Stop tossing me like cargo." She pulled away, her eyes red, her face defiant. "You left me!"

"No, I managed to get you on this train even though you left your post. I told you—"

"I had to use the bathroom! And how was I supposed to get home?"

The train lurched. People grabbed for whatever handholds they could find. Ula stumbled into Kol, quickly pushing away again. Her right sleeve slid to her wrist, exposing bare arm. "My best dress. They ripped it!"

He wrangled the sleeve back into place and held her shoulders, staring into her eyes. "I fell in love with you because you're smart and beautiful, but most of all because you're a fighter. I need someone next to me who's tough. I didn't want to leave, but you know I *have* to be on this train. There's a war going on. I've got a job to do."

Ula could feel the pinch of his two-fingered left hand. Funny, she hadn't noticed before now how different the grip felt than his five-fingered right hand.

"Listen to me." He squeezed a little harder and leaned closer. "I need you to use those smarts God gave you. We've got more rough water and bad skies ahead of us. You'll need to tack away from being a girl and tether in to being a woman. Can you do that for me?"

"Don't do it for *him*," drawled a woman standing in the landing. "Do it for yourself."

Ula shot her a daggered look. "Do you mind? This is a private conversation."

A half smirk turned the corner of the woman's mouth. "There's no privacy in war, sweetie."

"C'mon." Kol nudged Ula. "Let's find our seats." He squeezed past her, making a path down the crowded aisle.

Ula followed, as comments drifted behind her, "Baby war brides," and "That poor fellow." She pulled up her sleeve again and turned to glare, but people had already shuffled into the space where they'd been.

Another couple was sitting in their spot. "Sorry." The man stood, gathering his hat and coat. "My wife needed to rest her feet."

Ula flopped into the aisle seat he'd vacated—still warm and shaped to his body. Kol made a halting hand signal to the man's pregnant wife who was trying to push herself up. "Stay seated."

Ula looked at him. "But these were reserved seats."

"It's okay," Kol said.

"But I wanted to sit with *you*." Ula hadn't meant for a whine to tinge the last word.

"I'll take the armrest." He patted it, giving her a forced smile, then sat down and looked away.

Ula watched him. She'd done it again. What was she—twelve years old? Start acting like a woman, she chided herself.

A man in navy blues sat next to the window, filling out the row. Their seats faced three other women, who were already asking the big-bellied woman questions: *When are you due? What do you want—boy or girl? Where are you going?* Ula didn't care if the gal gave birth to a poodle. She'd never see any of these people again.

Kol sat on the armrest, rocking a baby as he talked to the father who was busy, wiping an older child's face. His back was to Ula; his long legs stretched across the aisle. She rubbed his shoulder and prepared to give him—according to her classmate, Tommy Jones—a smile that made angels sing. Kol didn't turn around.

Surely he was thinking she was a big mistake. She needed to look and act more adult. What did travelers who knew what they were doing look like? Gazing about the car for the first time, she saw that every seat was full; people sat in the aisles; others stood in the landings between cars. Many were servicemen in uniform, but most were couples or families with children parked on their laps.

Next to her, the pregnant woman was yammering, "There's no work in Arkansas." The other travelers murmured similar Depression woes. "So Ted is going to Seattle to get a job in the shipyards. His sister already works there as a welder."

Ula wondered what a woman could weld on a boat. Knobs? Railings? She'd heard women worked on airplanes too. Surely they hadn't built the B-25 that Joe flew. He'd sent a letter last week, saying his squadron was on the move, but he couldn't say where or when or even what the weather was like. "'Silence means security,' you know." Her father was praying it wasn't the European theatre. He didn't want Joe killing any relatives. Her mother was simply praying her son would return.

The lights dimmed in the train car. Ula kept her ripped sleeve pressed tightly to her side. The women across from her pulled out a blanket, and began opening it. They paused and offered it to the pregnant woman. She smiled and declined. They continued spreading it across their laps. Voices throughout the car lowered to a quiet murmur.

Night blacked out the windows. Ula wondered if the world had always been dark, and she hadn't known it. Maybe that's what her father was trying to protect her from. Her home now seemed like a tiny bubble of light in this chaotic, ugly darkness. She leaned her head back, trying to grasp images of the ruts under her swing, the warped steps to the porch, the pooched-out corner of the screen door where Joe had rammed it with his Radio Flyer.

Her eyes drifted shut. The rocking train drummed a steady cadence to her list of doubts. The magazines she and Patty had read made travel sound so exciting—but it wasn't. And marriage was so romantic—for about two hours—then it got iffy. She thumbed the wedding ring on her finger, then rested her palm on Kol's back to reassure herself he was really there. Voices seemed to hush then fade.

And the *Ladies' Home Journal* had promised that new places were opportunities for new friendships—but no one had befriended *her* with a blanket.

Secrets of the Toilet

Kol was gone again.

Ula awakened, leaned over the armrest, and peered up and down the aisle. People sat on the floor, propped against the sides of seats. The pregnant woman slept, open-mouthed, leaning against her. The two blanket-hogging women were still wrapped in their wool. The Navy man next to the window was looking out, using one finger to slightly push the shade away from the glass. Because no light was coming in, Ula assumed it was very early morning.

Abandoned again.

This time her stomach didn't clutch and her throat didn't close. Maybe it was the constant cradle-rock of the train. The car had taken on the scent of a basketball game at the Ponca City High School gym: bodies pressed together, topped with the remnants of food, and underlain with the sharp spike of adrenaline and change. It was both comforting and exciting. It made her both nervous and hungry.

Kol had to be somewhere on the train. She gently eased herself up, trying not to disturb the pregnant woman. Navigating the aisle was a bigger challenge. Grabbing the backs of seats, she anchored herself as she stepped over people. Here and there were small clutches of folks quietly talking. A couple of guys played poker, using their knees as a table. None of them wore a white hat.

Crossing from one car to the next was trying. Several people leaning against the walls of the landing had to move so she could get the door open. She hoped Kol hadn't taken off his cap. She'd never find him in these dark interiors. Slowly, she worked through five cars toward the end of the train. When she reached the last passenger car, she dreaded migrating back through the bodies so she could check the front. Knowing Kol, he was in the locomotive, chatting with the engineer. He seemed to have that kind of charisma. Even her father had enjoyed their spirited debates, though she doubted he'd act charitably toward him now.

Her chest tightened with the thought of her parents. Tears pushed into her eyes. She hurried through the restroom door at the end of the car. A tall woman seated on the toilet looked up. "Oh! Sorry!" Ula gasped.

"No, hon." The woman stood. "I'm just resting here. It's the only open seat on the train."

"Sorry." Ula's eyes squinched tight, squeezing back tears as she backed out the door. "I'm looking for—" her voice cracked with a half sob.

"Oh hon, get in here." The woman pulled at Ula's arm, yanking off her sleeve again. "Oh crap! How'd that happen? I'm so sorry. Sit down. I'll fix it."

"Not your fault," Ula blubbered, aware how pathetic her shudders sounded, but she couldn't stop them.

"Sit down. Have a good cry. That's what toilets are for."

Ula tore off toilet paper and daubed her eyes.

"This war-time toilet paper..." The woman let out a disgusted sigh as she pulled a sewing packet from her purse. "It's like wiping yourself with sweater fuzz."

Ula snorted a laugh. Snot bubbled from her nose. She scratched a wad of paper from the roll and blew. "I ran away with a man," she blurted. The lady cast a glance at Ula, then her eyes returned to threading her needle. It was a worldly glance. The kind that says...*well, I can tell you how this story ends, but you go on.* Ula swallowed. "Now he thinks I'm too young."

"How old are you?"

"Eighteen." Ula wasn't sure why she'd lied. All she knew was that she didn't want this elegant, stylish woman to think she was a child.

"That's not too young. How old is he?"

"Twenty-eight."

"Oh. An older man, huh? And he thinks he has more worldly experience? Been around a bit more?"

"He does. He's in the Merchant Marine." Ula snuffled, looking at the floor.

"Well that's fixable, hon. Now hold still. Let me tack your sleeve in place." She bent over Ula's shoulder. "First time I was with a man, I bawled like a cow afterward. Men hate that. You think maybe you cry a little too much?"

"I can't stop. I want to act more grown up. I don't know how." Ula smeared a tear off her cheek. "Back home, I was more mature than any of the girls in my class, but now…. Am I supposed to act nice and fawn over the folks who took our seats? Or to the guys that pawed me, getting me onto the train?" Another rack of sobs shook her. "I wasn't raised like this," she said in-between gasps. "Really. I'm not a bad person."

"Of course you aren't, hon." The woman looked Ula in the eyes. "You're just scared. Everything is new and different. Tell me your name."

"Eulalia. But everybody calls me Ula. Like ooooo-la-la."

"Well! That's memorable. There. Done." The woman smiled at the few Frankenstein stitches she'd put at the top of the sleeve. "Ula, I'm Melody. Wash your face." She pointed to the sink. "My real name is Martha," she said as Ula splashed water on her eyes. "But I introduce myself as Melody because that's who I want to be now."

"You just changed your name? What does your family call you?"

"Who cares? There's a war on. Everything and everybody is changing. You've got to get over crying about that, or you'll be bawling all the time."

"I don't know how to be a war bride. It's not like *Vogue* makes it out to be. I know what the commandments teach and how my mother acted. But she was never manhandled at a train station or got ditched by her husband."

"Oh, you don't know what happened when she was young. She could surprise you. Dry your face and do your lips." Melody gracefully pointed toward the fabric looping from the towel machine. In the other manicured hand she held out a gold tube of lipstick. "That's the first thing you've gotta change—your expectations."

"This is red," Ula said, looking inside the tube. "My father is a pastor, so I've never worn anything this bright. I don't think my husband would like it."

"I thought you said you wanted to be grown up?" Melody leveled a stare at the young woman. "I don't know what you thought being with a man was like, but those magazines and your mama didn't tell you the real nitty gritty."

"Like what?"

"Do your lips and sit down, hon. You just enrolled in the Melody Markett Crash Course for War Brides."

How To Keep A Man

*I*n rapid fire, Melody handed out advice. "Let him order for you in a restaurant. If you can cook, do it—men love to be taken care of. Put him in charge of directions when you go anywhere."

Ula didn't hear the rest; she was memorizing Melody's hand movements and the way she looked. How did she get a dress like that in wartime? Her mother would say it wasn't a daytime color. Bold red flowers splayed across a white background with short flutter sleeves that floated each time Melody moved her arms. Her neckline veed to a tempting spot just above her bosom where a trail of buttons pulled the eye to her form-fitted waist. And the skirt was a wonder—full of fabric hanging in soft, lovely folds. Ula guessed she made up for the extra fabric usage by making the skirt shorter, falling slightly higher than the knees—the mandated wartime length lest anyone use too much material. Her hair curled to her shoulders, topped by a smart red hat with a blue feather. But it was her shoes that Ula coveted. Peep-toed wedgies in red, white, and blue leather. A single strap circled Melody's slim ankle.

Ula glanced at her own frog-grain Oxfords with flat wooden soles. With all leather going for army boots, she hadn't had new shoes in two years—only hand-me downs from the church ladies. That's what she needed to look more grown up. Shoes like those and a bit more leg showing. She had nice legs. She flounced the hem of her cotton dress, smoothing it, so it barely covered her knees as she sat.

"Are you listening?" Melody tapped a red polished nail against Ula's forehead as though she were knocking.

"I love your shoes. Are they real leather?"

"Heaven help you, hon. How long have you been off the farm?"

Ula looked at her watch. "We left about four hours ago."

"Holy bells!"

The restroom door rattled.

Melody yelled at the door. "Go to another one, please. We're cleaning in here." Ula gave her a quizzical frown. "Look at me, hon. We need to wrap this up. There's only one thing you need to know to keep your fella happy. First of all, forget all that junk you've read in magazines or True Romance novels. Are you listening?"

Ula nodded.

"You need to remember—always make your man feel like a man. That's it." She shrugged. "Admire the manly things about him. Don't try to change him. People change, but not according to plan. Men want to feel loved." She flexed a bicep. "To feel needed."

"The last time I needed him, he wasn't anywhere around. I don't even know where he is now."

"Well if you ever find him, thank him." Melody held up a hand to stave off the questions forming on Ula's lips. "It doesn't have to be for anything special. Everyday things like opening a door. Or fixing something. Tell him you're thankful to have a man who watches over you. You do that and I *gar-ron-tee* he'll die trying to take care of you."

Ula looked skeptical.

"Look, hon, why don't you go home? Wait for him. Work on some of this stuff."

"I'll lose him. I doubt if any more dream-boat, dark-haired Captains will come to my little burg."

"A Merchant Marine?"

"Yeah?"

"You caught a sheik, hon. Better pay attention to the guy if you don't want him to abandon ship. I ran into him earlier."

"Where?" Ula quickly stood up.

"Whoa, hon."

"Where?" Ula demanded.

The door rattled.

"Just a minute," Melody called to the door then faced Ula again. "Listen, I don't know what your mother told you about sex, but I'm telling you it's okay to enjoy yourself. You don't have to do anything. Just moan. He'll feel like a stallion."

Ula drew back slightly, her eyebrows disappearing into her hairline. "We haven't...had...relations."

"Oh hell!" Melody leaned her head back, rolling her eyes. "You have a diaphragm don't you?"

Ula slowly shook her head.

Someone knocked and jiggled the handle.

"Cross your legs and hold it!" Melody bellowed at the door. "We've got a damn emergency in here!" Ula winced and moved away. Melody gripped her arm. "You need to get to a doctor and be fitted for a diaphragm. It'll keep you from having babies."

"But I want babies." Ula took small side steps toward the door, tugging Melody with her.

"No, you don't. Not for a year at least. Trust me. If you get pregnant right now, you'll be wearing shoes like that," Melody pointed at Ula's feet, "for the rest of your life."

Ula stared at her black, square-toed clod-hoppers next to Melody's strappy, sexy wedges. Heaven help her, but she really wanted those shoes. She jerked as Melody pinched her arm.

"Promise me! You're a preacher's kid. You've gotta keep your promises. Tell me you'll get a diaphragm before you screw around. There's already enough 'goodbye babies' from this war."

Ula nodded, the red of her cheeks, mottling into the whitish shock around her eyes. The world was indeed a black cauldron of sin. If her father were here, she'd apologize for her trouble-making. Sorry, Papa...I didn't know.

Two hard knocks were followed by a male voice. "This is the conductor. Is everything all right? I have someone here to assist you."

Melody grabbed the door handle before Ula could. "Hold up. I want to give you something." She pulled a small square of white silk trimmed in yellow lace from her purse. "Here." She held it by a corner, letting it drape in soft folds. "It's a magic hankie. It stops tears." She pushed it into Ula's palm.

"I...don't think—" Ula started.

But Melody had already turned the knob. A black maid and a conductor filled the doorway. A woman with a baby on her hip peeked over their shoulders.

"Sorry for the inconvenience." Melody's voice was deep and breathy. "Hopefully we averted a crisis. Loose lips. That sort of thing." She winked holding a *shhhh* finger in front of her full pagoda-red lips.

The conductor and maid squeezed past to look inside.

Melody whispered, "Your fella?" She gave Ula a knowing look, hooking her thumb toward the baggage compartment. Ula took off, bumping into people.

"Whoa." Melody grabbed a handful of Ula's skirt. A couple of stitches popped as Ula strained to hurry down the aisle. "Sorry, hon. All your buttons in place?" Melody pretended to check as she stepped next to Ula and whispered, "Slow down! Don't go rushing in like a thirsty cow going to the waterhole. Just open the door, stick your head in, and glance around. If you see him, ignore him. Close the door and leave. Be a wifely queen. Make Prince Charming chase after you. Remember," she tapped a toe forward, turning her foot side to side, showing off a delicate, shapely ankle. "This is who you are inside, Cinderella."

Ula gave a single determined nod, staring at the platform shoe. She felt two pats on her shoulder and heard Melody whisper behind her, "Go make him happy. Or go home, kid." Then she received a push.

Taking slow, careful steps, Ula worked her way between people until she stood in front of the door. Holding her breath, she opened it and peeked in.

Lutherans, Liver Loaf,
And A Lotta Leg

U la had expected to see suitcases neatly stacked like the
hat box display at Lee's department store in Ponca City.
Instead, piles of packages, crates, and canvas duffels littered
the baggage compartment. One small light, protected by a
metal cage, shone from the ceiling. At the opposite end of the
car, a red bulb cast an eerie glow over a man sleeping on slatted
boxes. As instructed, she ignored him, casually continuing her
scan of the car. She was about to close the door when her eye
caught a swatch of something white to her immediate right. On
top of a stack of flat-topped coffins lay a man stretched out on
his back. Ula drew a sharp breath, seeing a white military hat
covering his face.

Slowly, she backed away and quietly pulled the door shut.
She turned, frantically looking for Melody. The floral dress, red
hat, and strappy platforms were nowhere in sight. Of course,
when she needed someone—they weren't there.

The people in the aisle swayed slightly with the beat of the
train's wheels. Folks in their seats were yawning and awaken-
ing. A few had snapped the shades up on their windows. A
mother cut cubes of Liver Loaf, using a paper sack as her
tablecloth. She handed them one by one to her children who
popped them in their mouths. The little boy dropped one. "Pick
it up and eat it," the mother told him. He did. "Bleech!" said his
older sister and received a swat from her mom.

It was strange how life could be so normal here and so...half
worldly through the door behind her. Ula pressed her fingertips
to her eyes and rubbed. She scanned again for Melody, but the

car had the feeling of day to day life—not the breath-holding anticipation that someone would heroically arrive to save her or teach her. Not even the conductor or maid was around.

Moving slowly, she slipped back into the baggage car, trying not to make a sound. The body on top of the coffin wasn't wearing a blue jacket with gold braiding. Just a white pressed shirt and blue slacks. Ula watched his chest for a long time, but the dim light and rocking train didn't reveal a rise and fall.

She looked for something to poke him with so she didn't have to get close, but all she had was the silk hankie she still clutched. Carefully, she neared the body. The hat seemed right, though she couldn't see the insignia. As she reached to lift it a smidge, the joggling of the train made her brush the man's stubbly chin. The body didn't move. Ula didn't either, craning her neck to peek at the face.

"Whaddyadoin!" He swiftly gripped her wrist, jerking her down.

She shrieked and pulled away. His other hand grabbed her, dragging her until they were nose to nose. "Welcome to cargo, lassie," he growled in a pirate voice.

Ula gawked. In less than an eye blink, her surprise turned to relief as she stared at Kol. Then her face flashed a fiery wrath. "That's not funny!"

From the back of the car, the man on top of the crates drawled, "Ya okay, lady?"

"Shhhh. Shhhh," Kol soothed her. "Don't wake everyone up. C'mon...it *is kinda* funny."

"Let me go," Ula twisted her arm, her voice hot with threat.

"I'm sorry I scared you. At sea we pull pranks all the time. Relieves the boredom. I guess you haven't seen that side of me. It didn't seem appropriate to joke around at your father's house." He let go of her.

She took a step back, running her hands over her skirt, brushing out imaginary wrinkles and the last wisps of fear. She cleared her throat but didn't look at him. "I'm supposed to do a better job of thanking you." Her voice cracked as though the words hurt. "So...thank you for being strong and scary. I hate you." She turned and walked out.

"Ula!" He rushed from the baggage car, calling down the aisle. Heads turned, looking at him then tracking her as she weaved through people. "It was a joke. Ula! You'll laugh at this when we're old." His face fell and shoulders slumped as he followed her. This wasn't the first time in the last four hours he'd wondered what he'd gotten into. The debates with her dad had been enjoyable—even though he was a rough ol' bluenose. And so far, this was the first girl he'd met who'd been raised to use her brain instead of giggle and bat her eyes. He'd spent seven days at their house and had never gotten bored. A gal who said what she thought and who had a strong spine wouldn't be waiting by the time the war ended. He was sure he'd better snap her up quick. He'd never figured she could start wars all by herself.

Ahead of him, a man was ignoring Ula's attempts to get past. She ducked under his arm and pushed through. In a few more feet, she stepped over people, stumbling when they didn't move their legs in time. At the end of the car, a pot-bellied man with a large, red-veined nose lounged against the door. "Could you step aside?" Ula demanded.

"Sure. Sure." He smiled and stretched as a prelude to moving. "You know I had a dog once. A setter. Pretty thing, but wouldn't come when I called it."

"I can see why," Ula said.

Kol slipped his arm around Ula's shoulder. "Thanks, bud, I've got this." He urged her to turn and go back down the aisle.

"No problem." The fat man called after him. "A few whacks oughta straighten her out. Did for my dog."

Ula stiffened and hesitated. Kol's hand nudged her forward. She didn't want to go anywhere with him, but judging from the way people moved and let them pass, their little spat had been entertainment for the whole car. He'd chased her, but it wasn't what she'd planned. Heat rose in her cheeks and she hurried forward. It wasn't Lutheran to draw attention to yourself.

Faces turned as they passed. She couldn't wait to hide in the twilight world of the baggage car. Then kick Kol for putting her through this.

As soon as they were past the door, she whirled to face him. "You left me—again!"

"That armrest was slicing the cheeks off my backside. You were asleep. If you'd stayed where you were supposed to, I would've been back to get you. Like I tried to do at the train station. I'm used to giving orders, and those orders being obeyed."

"Well, I'm not used to taking orders."

"Hah! With a father like yours? He marched you and your mother around fifty times a day." Kol lowered his voice in a gruff imitation of Pastor Haupt. "We'll have dinner at five. I have an Elder's meeting at six. Don't buy any more of this oleo-stuff. It tastes like something a Frenchman would wear."

"Those weren't orders. That's his personality."

"So I said to myself, Kol, this gal knows how to put up with a lot of crap and dance around it without getting her shoes dirty. Guess I was wrong."

"You left me for the second time in four hours."

"And you left me."

They stared at each other. A voice rasped through the dusky quietness of the car, "Why don't cha both leave? I'm tryin' to sleep here."

The Captain snorted a quiet chuckle. Ula tried to hold a stern face, but it crumbled. He pulled her to his chest. "Tell you what, if one of us goes somewhere, we'll leave a message for the other. Deal?"

"How am I supposed to do that? Send a telegram? Scratch it on a wall?"

"Tell someone. Leave a note. Can you imagine my surprise when I came to see you this morning and found an ugly ol' guy with a missing ear?"

"I must've been in the bathroom getting this." She held up her hankie. "And instructions on how to make a man happy."

"Yeah? What were they?"

"You'll have to wait and see. Right now I'm hungry and tired."

"We change trains in Dallas. Maybe we'll have time to grab something there. Care to join me on a casket for now?"

"Creepers. No! That's tempting fate."

"They're empty." He lifted her on top. "There's nothing inside, I checked." He hopped on the adjoining coffin, lay down, and drew her next to him.

She sighed. Nothing was turning out right. She felt cheated. Her first time lying in the forbidden full-frontal hug with a man—and it was on top of a coffin. That couldn't bode well. She sure wasn't telling Patty about this either.

"Now, show me some of that how-to-make-your-man happy advice." He pulled her closer.

She looked up as though the list was written in the top of her skull. "I'm supposed to appreciate you and say stuff like thank you for not leaving me at the station."

"That's it? Who's giving out these tips?"

"Some lady in the bathroom."

"A tall gal, flashy dress and red hat?"

"That's Melody, well her name's Martha but—"

"Nice looking gal? A lotta leg?" He propped himself on one elbow to look at her. Ula nodded. "She's a hooker." Seeing confusion on Ula's face he added, "A prostitute."

"No!" Ula shook her head so hard she almost fell off the coffin. "She was nice. Told me about lipstick, shoes, said I should make you food, and to thank you for everything."

"Well, she offered to teach me something about sex." Kol put a finger over Ula's lips, momentarily hushing her. "I said no. What did she tell you?"

"To moan and call you a stallion." They stared at each other, an embarrassing silence wrapping around them.

Across the room a voice rasped, "I'm all for that one."

Seattle, The Emerald City

T he train traveled across the state of Arizona before they finally got to sit together. Ula had awakened one time and found Kol's seat empty, but there was a scribbled note, *Gone to smoke.* She hated his pipe. He was always plugging it, scraping it, or knocking it against something. That would have to go.

When they finally exited the train in Seattle, the depot pulsed with chaos and hurry. Kol ushered her to a spot by the door. "Stay right here." He pointed to a poster of Uncle Sam floating like a god on clouds, admonishing everyone to *Buy War Bonds!* "I need to check with freight. The ship may be loading tonight."

Ula sat on her suitcase, her finger tracing a crack in its side that had started in Oklahoma City when she'd stood on it. She and her luggage had never been so far from home. From the looks of the people in the station, neither had they. Some faces wore blank, worried looks of where-to-go and what-to-do-next. Others rushed by, their footsteps close to another's heels, bodies leaning forward as though the future was a headwind to be plowed through.

Shortly, Kol returned with a grin, pulling her to her feet and nudging her toward the exit. "I don't have to get underway yet. I won't leave until tomorrow. The night is ours."

"Wait a minute!" Ula stopped walking. "You're leaving tomorrow?"

He went past, casting a backward glance as he parted the throng, her suitcase in one hand, his duffel over his shoulder. "Ula, don't you understand we're at war? C'mon."

No. She didn't understand. The war in Oklahoma had never been like this. Oh...they had meatless Tuesdays and scrap drives to do their part, but these convulsing mobs of dashing people, eating off their laps, and laying plans by war's stopwatch didn't exist. In Ponca, families still ate together—at a table. And prayed for those who were absent.

"Hurry! Before it leaves." Kol trotted into the night.

"You're leaving tomorrow?" Ula followed in a dumb stupor, dashing from the depot into a deluge of rain. He helped her squeeze into an already-full street car.

Ula had never been on one. And she still didn't know what it looked like. All she could see were people packed in a box. Some sat in seats, most hung onto straps. The driver was a man, but the conductorettes, taking tickets in their green uniforms, were girls who looked her age.

Kol grabbed her hand and placed it on an overhead strap. "Seattle's a beautiful city. You'll like it."

"If you can see it through the rain," a man added. Water dripped from his fedora and trickled down the shoulders of his heavy jacket.

Ula glared. Didn't anyone have the manners to stay out of another person's conversation? The car moved forward, knocking her into the wet man, her hand grabbing for air. "Sorry. Sorry," was all she ended up saying instead of "Mind your own business."

By the time they transferred to the third street car, the florets of Ula's bra were outlined through her wet, cotton dress. She shivered as Kol slipped his coat around her, murmuring, "It won't be long now." Crimson flushed her cheeks. She pulled the jacket closer.

They got off, stepping over broken bottles and sidewalks with missing bricks. Kol held the suitcase over their heads as they walked several blocks. "A pal told me about this place." His voice pitched with excitement. "We'll be lucky if we can get it. Say a prayer—or two." His words and his stride sped up. Ula kept pace, staring at the rain bouncing hard off the bricks, and wishing a bitter farewell to her lost sleeve. It had ripped off again and was now riding one of the street cars. This had been her best dress.

The living space Kol had found was over a neighborhood bar. Mirrors and wallpaper were evidence that at one time a family had lived there and cared for the place. Now each room housed boarders, like many of the buildings in the area.

"We are s-o-o-o-o fortunate to get this." He dropped the suitcase and duffel to the floor with a *thump*.

Ula looked at the sparse furniture in the room: a dresser, oval mirror, armoire, and a bed that seemed to be growing bigger by the minute. "Where do you usually stay?"

"Closer to the docks. Not as nice or safe."

Ula gave him a look. She couldn't imagine a dumpier place. There was no grass or flowers in the neighborhood. People slept in doorways, and at this luxury inn, which didn't include meals, the walls were mottled with water stains and the paper peeled from the corners.

"Why don't you get out of those wet clothes?" He began to lift his jacket from her shoulders.

Ula put a pincer grip on the front and pulled it to her body. "Where's the bathroom?"

Kol kept his hands on the jacket. He watched Ula switch her stare between the door and her sodden feet. "Down the hall. Tell you what..." he gave her a peck on the cheek and walked to the door. "How about a little privacy? I need a smoke and to pick up some things."

When he'd returned an hour later, he opened the door to see Ula sitting on the bed, fully clothed. Her wet dress and under garments were nowhere in sight. He suspected she'd packed them. "I come bearing gifts." He pulled a couple of ham sandwiches and a bottle of gin out of a bag. Ula didn't say anything. "And you're still here. That's a good start."

"What's this about leaving tomorrow?" Her shoes were anchored to the mattress rail; her hands gripped the edge of the bed. "And I don't drink."

Kol let out the sigh of a man who's aware he has a long night ahead. "I know." He filled a glass to the brim. "It's for me."

When the deed was done, Ula said she didn't see what the big hoopla was. Sex was just a raw sensation and a lot of grunting. She thought it might've been different if she'd moaned, but she'd forgotten. When he rolled onto his back, she'd asked, "That's it?"

"It gets better." He sighed, his eyes closed.

"You're a stallion."

He choked, coughing on a laugh, and then drew her to him, falling asleep within moments.

In two hours, he was awake, packing his duffel, putting on his still-damp jacket. "I'll be back in three weeks. We're—"

"No." Her eyes flashed wide. "Where will you be? Does this have to do with that shipment on the train?"

"I can't say, and you can't tell anyone what little you know, understand? Not a word. But I'll be back."

"You can't go. Not after what we just did. You can't leave me like this."

"I wish I didn't have to." Half of the gin and most of the night were gone by the time he'd convinced her to remove all of her clothes and answered her questions: Will you love me forever? Will you still respect me? Will it hurt? How does the rubber thing work? Where'd you get it? And did anyone see you buying it?

"Don't go," she'd begged again, clutching the sheet to her bare chest as she sat up in bed.

"I'm sorry. You know I've got to. You said you wanted to get away from your dad's dictatorship—be treated like an adult. I told you I'd be gone a lot. You said you'd wait forever. We talked about this." She gave a little nod.

He hefted his bag onto his shoulder. "I left you some spending money. Don't go down to the docks. If anyone bothers you, don't tell them I'll punch their teeth in when I get back. It only lets them know you're alone right now. I've hired a woman to check on you every day. Her name is Mrs. Bomkamp. You'll be safe here."

"You'll come back? Promise? You won't leave me stranded?"

"Watch for me." He pointed toward the window, gave her a kiss, and then went out the door.

That had been a week ago. She'd found the note he'd left on the dresser. *I love you.* Well, he was Lutheran—and Norwegian—she didn't expect him to be blubbery but a bit more sentiment would've been nice.

After two weeks, it wasn't the cussing next door that bothered Ula. It was the silence. Her little room in the boarding house felt more like a hidey-hole than a honeymoon suite. She never left it, but preferred watching the street from her window. The men in rooms on either side of her were crude and loud when awake. The old house's floors creaked. The walls barely filtered noise. The armoire was shallow. She had to slant the hangers of her two dresses diagonally to close the door, but she could sit inside of it. She'd tried already—twice since Kol had left.

***

Ula now understood why new kids at her parochial school had acted like lost chickens. They had sidled along the walls of the hallway, stumped by the simplest decisions: who to talk to or where to sit. Of course, she hadn't publicly made fun of them, but wearing her comfort-with-her-surroundings like a queen's cape, she'd secretly rolled her eyes at them. Never before had she been the outsider. Everyone in Ponca knew her—or her father.

In Seattle, Ula spent day after day trying to shake off a thick blanket of fear. The men on the street wore layers of dirty clothes and walked with a slouched shuffle. The browbeaters next door scuffed around, using a universal man-language, putting *goddamn* or *helluva* in front of every noun.

Mrs. Bomkamp, a round-faced fish seller, had visited once or twice a week. She never failed to tell Ula how lucky she was to have a whole room, explaining that most of the boarders were hot bedding. So when the sheet metal men from Boeing got off work, they slipped into the recently vacated beds of other shift workers.

"Then how do they have time for all the cussing I hear through the walls?" Ula watched the red-cheeked woman unpack a greasy packet of smoked fish and hard discs of pilot bread.

"That's probably from the pipefitters on the other side of ya. Don't go traipsin' about in yer bathrobe when they're around. Them shipyard apes are a rough lot. Probably learned some new words, ain't ya?" Mrs. Bomkamp winked, gouging Ula in the ribs with her elbow.

"I hardly leave the room. I pee in a pot and dump it when everyone's asleep. Why aren't you coming every day, and why haven't you brought the fabric I asked for?"

"Listen, Lady Astor," the gap-toothed woman scowled. "Some of us're doin' real work. There's a war goin' on. You can't get any of that material now. And don't you go lookin' for it. Little bird like you would disappear from the market in an hour."

Often, there were long stretches of silence when everyone but Ula had something to do. She'd written letters. Several to her mother, saying she was fine. One to Patty, bragging about being a war bride. But Joe was her lifeline. Each day she spilled her heart to him on paper. How stupid she'd been, thinking the world was like Ponca, and that being married meant wearing aprons, fixing toast, and enduring a husband's crotchety rants like their mom had. She'd end each letter with *Don't tell Mom. She's already on her knees, constantly praying for you.*

Kol had returned as promised, and then left again. He had ships to pilot and a war that kept pushing him around. No amount of begging, threatening, or cussing with her newfound vocabulary motivated him to find a town job. "You're my only love," he'd assured her. "I'll always come back to you." Yet he spent most of his time with his mistress, the sea.

She stared out the window, tapping the wedding ring on her finger with the one piece of V-Mail she'd received from her brother. A hastily scribbled note: *Go home.*

How could she? She was a shameful humiliation. What if she left and Kol never returned to Oklahoma to get her? Not even the dull-witted farmer boys would ask her out for a Dr. Pepper. She'd be evidence that Pastor Haupt couldn't control his own family. He'd be pastor of a deflowered daughter who'd dumped her husband and a murdering son that went overseas to slaughter his relatives.

Kol was wrong. If he'd truly loved her, he should've left her in Oklahoma. She would have waited—probably. Well...maybe not if she'd known this was what sex and marriage were like.

The bed made a creaking complaint as she got off of it. She hated the damn bed. It announced when she got up, when she slept, and each time Kol came home. And she certainly had never taken the opportunity to moan while in it.

She was a prisoner here, dithering between her fear of being raped and her desperate longing to talk to someone. It was supposed to be different. She thought she'd be sewing curtains and trying out recipes in the *Home Journal*—not collecting profanity in a flop house. Kol was an idiot for bringing her here.

He was also head of their household. Almost seventeen years as a pastor's kid had drilled into her a duty: obey your husband.

However, she'd already broken the fourth commandment when she'd eloped: Honor your father and mother.

Actually, she'd broken so many commandments; she wasn't quite sure where she stood anymore.

She'd dishonored everyone, including herself. She couldn't go home, but staying was torture.

With a quick prayer, she shakily pinned on her hat and put her only other dress—missing a sleeve—in her suitcase.

Taking a big breath and exhaling another quick prayer, she closed her eyes and hurried through the door. God help her, but she was going to break another commandment.

For the second time in her life she ran away.

One Dress For Work, One For Show

*U*la stood at the steps of The Sisters of the Holy Trail, tears streaming down her cheeks, blood trickling from her nose, dripping off her chin. "Please don't send me away."

An old nun, eyes wide, beckoned her inside. The wrinkle-faced Sister pointed to a hallway bench and left. Shortly, she returned with a wet cloth. A younger Sister, wearing black horn-rimmed glasses, coaxed enough words from Ula to understand that her husband had left her at an unsavory boarding house, and she'd bolted, falling down the stairs. Now she was searching for refuge.

When Ula was able to draw a breath without sobbing and her nose dribbling, she was put in a tiny cell-like room with a narrow pine dresser and a slender bed against the wall. It made her flophouse room seem palatial in size. It also made it seem as noisy as a train station. The silence here was deep and layered.

A quick *rap-rap* made Ula start. The door opened and a short nun in a mid-calf habit and thick black stockings beckoned.

Ula followed, passing a tiny Christmas tree with homemade ornaments in the stone-tiled hallway. "Is it Christmas yet? I didn't see anyone outside my window carrying presents or a tree. I've lost track of days. I...I've been..."

The nun walked on, keeping her steady waddling pace, favoring her right leg.

"I'm Eulalia." She ran several steps to catch up. "I'm sorry if I bothered anyone. I didn't know where to go. I followed the sound of your bells." The nun nodded with a non-committal smile, which showed about the same amount of pleasure as a good tooth-brushing at the end of the night.

The Sister stopped, pointing for Ula to enter an oak-walled study. Between piles of books and folders on a desk, a nun looked up, her white coif covering everything except her face under a black veil.

Ula dipped a slight curtsey. She had no idea how to greet an important nun. The only practices she knew were the sign of the cross and counting beads. Both rituals seemed wrong for this situation.

"I'm Mother Radagunda. Please sit."

Ula lowered onto a short wooden stool, mesmerized by the Sister's old-soul eyes staring out of a wrinkle-free face.

The nun spoke slowly as though a weight pulled at each word. "I understand you are in a bit of a straight and have requested a place to stay?"

"Oh, yes, ma'am, please?" Ula dry-washed her hands.

The Mother stared until Ula stopped shifting on the wooden stool and stilled her hands. "You have arrived at a rather challenging time for us. Perhaps it was meant to be a fortuitous moment for you. Usually, our Novices and Candidates maintain the cleanliness of Holy Trail House, but many of the young women during this war have chosen to pledge themselves to the Women's Army Corp or the Women Air Force Service Pilots rather than to God. Sister Heavé is in need of help with the daily meals and kitchen cleaning. The woman who previously performed these services for the Lord took a job at Boeing. If you are willing to serve in this manner, we could supply a bed, meals, and a very small stipend. However, if your husband comes home from sea, you will not be able to entertain him here."

Ula nodded.

The Mother's voice rose an octave which made it seem like she was shouting, "Additionally, you will not disturb our Sacred

Silence. Many in our community observe serenity and have little need for chatter. If you are disruptive, you will leave."

"I'm quiet as air." Ula began wringing her hands again. "I don't know how to say this, but...do I have to become Roman Catholic? My dad's a Lutheran pastor, and he'd disown me if I ever became a Catholic or a nun."

The words hung between them. Ula stared at the floor, suddenly aware she'd stripped away any veneer of hospitality or thankfulness. An uncomfortable minute passed until the Mother finally spoke, "You will be required to attend evening Compline. It is not necessary that you convert to Catholicism, but I ask that you keep an open heart as you work here." The Sister started to say more but closed her eyes, tapping her finger against her lips. Silence reigned again for as long as it took a few raindrops outside to fall from heaven and splat the earth. She opened her eyes. "As for being a nun...I think that ship has sailed." She nodded at the back of the room. The Sister in horn-rimmed glasses moved from her unseen corner, spooking Ula. With a shoulder tap, Ula was ushered from the oak-walled study.

That evening, the deep sleep of relief came quickly, but at three o'clock, she awakened, listening for the familiar curses and squeaking beds of the shift workers. The only sound drifting into her basement space was the gargling echo of a rain pipe outside the building.

Her room was even smaller than the one she had seen upstairs. She had to put her hand on the floor and brace herself when she turned over to make sure she didn't fall off the narrow bench-like bed and straw-filled mattress. Without windows, the blackness around her carried the weight and smell of dead air.

In the morning, she reported to Sister Heavé. The pudgy, bug-eyed mistress of the kitchen had more rules than a British general. "You will only speak to a Sister if spoken to. You will *not* speak to the Candidates or Novices. You will—"

"How do I tell the difference?" Steam fogged Ula's face as she stirred a big pot of oatmeal.

"Heaven help us!" Sister Heavé rolled her eyes and then checked the twenty pieces of toast in the oven. She spoke to the ceiling as though God reclined on the purlin rafters, legs crossed, smoking a cigar, and listening for prayers. "*This* is what you send me?" The nun waggled a hot pad at Ula. "Girl, climb that ladder and get the brown sugar off the top shelf. I have to hide it, or Sister Willfreeda will be at it with a spoon. I'll need your ration book too."

"My name is Ula." Her words snapped with irritation as she went up an old wooden step-stool. "And I don't have a ration book."

"Saints preserve us!" The Sister gave the ceiling a you've-got-to-be-kidding look. "Well, *dummchen*, how do you expect to eat if you don't have rations? And don't let that pot burn." Ula paused in a crouch, unsure whether to dive and rescue the oatmeal or continue the hunt for brown sugar.

Over the next few days, Ula guessed that Sister Heavé, whom she'd secretly nicknamed Plumpy, must be a lost relative. Like her father, the Sister had a bucket of rants and a pot-load of complaints that God wasn't working on fast enough. Ula put her sixteen-some years of living with her dad to use by tuning out the nun.

Unlike her father, there were no meetings, raised voices, or desk thumping. It confused her that events at the cloister progressed quietly and orderly. Hell, Ula thought, these women barely speak to each other. How do they know who's supposed to do what?

And why was it so hard for her to quit cussing? She'd lived sixteen years without profanity. In the span of two months she'd learned the musical beat of swearing. Now, without a thought, it seemed to find a rhythm in her sentences.

After lunch on the third day, Sister Heavé told her to clean up and present herself to Mother Radagunda.

"Why?"

"God doesn't deign to tell man everything, and the Mother isn't obliged to tell me *anything*. So I don't know. It's none of my affair."

Ula shook her head, amazed that a few days ago, she'd been desperate for company. Now she wished Sister Plumpy would take a vow of silence.

The next day, the Sister asked, "And what did the Mother want with you, *dummchen*?"

"What is that? A dumpling?" Ula glanced up from stirring a white sauce and saw the nun shrug. "If you must know, we went to a bar and had a beer."

"The cheek!" Sister Heavé raised a wooden spoon then paused. With a sad, wishful look for the old days of swacking the sass out of a young'un, she smacked it against the stone counter. "It's shameful you'd say such things after Mother took you in when your husband left you. Impertinence will cost you a week on your hands and knees, scouring ovens, floors, and steps."

"Sorry." Ula whipped the sauce, scowling at Plumpy, who seemed to get her panties in a twist over the silliest things. Nobody would believe these dried-up nuns would swig a beer. "The Mother accompanied me to the boarding house. I left a note to tell my husband—who didn't abandon me. He's at sea right now—" Ula stuck her chin out. "To let him know where I am in case he makes it home for Christmas."

58

It had been Mother Radagunda's idea. She'd reminded Ula that the bond of matrimony was sacred. It was Ula's holy duty to honor her husband, *especially* because he was busy fighting a war.

Ula had agreed half-heartedly. The Mother asked to read her note, and after a few shame-inducing suggestions, Ula made corrections—such as writing more than just the convent's name. The Mother insisted on accompanying her, "to ensure you're safe while delivering it."

Ula was embarrassed for the nun to see the decaying room and the bed which seemed as big as an elephant. Of course, leaving the message was the right thing to do. And yet...Ula's stomach sloshed with guilt...she wasn't sure she wanted Kol to find her. The longer she had looked out the flophouse window for him, the more childish their relationship felt.

"It took that long to deliver a note?" Sister Heavé interrupted Ula's thoughts, scraping a chopped onion into the pot. "You were gone several hours."

Ula beat the sauce faster. "I thought you didn't care. But it'll tickle whatever you wear beneath that habit to know we also picked up a ration book for me."

"Praise the Lord! More victuals. And may He work the guff out of you." The sister shook her head. "The day you came out of heaven, you must've snatched the whole lot of impertinence! I'll pray for you in Compline."

Ula put on the rueful face she'd seen on Novices. She'd say a prayer too—for herself—because she was forced to attend Compline every night.

Christmas Day brought a liturgical change in music and a special caramel bread pudding for the community. That was all. Ula lay in her bed that night, remembering the candlelight of past church services. One of the organ's keys always stuck.

Everyone held the last note of *Silent Night* on each chorus until the organist could flick it loose. And old lady Braun would yodel the high, Gloria notes in *Angels We Have Heard on High*, causing guests to turn around and look.

Lying in the dark, Ula explored the emptiness inside of her. Kol hadn't come. She hadn't really expected him. After all, she'd run away. But a tiny part hoped he'd show up. She would give him hell for carting her from her home then leaving her at the worst Christmas in her life.

She'd found a pair of knitted blue slippers on her pillow this evening. It was such a little thing, but it filled her beggarly holiday. She thanked Plumpy, who waved her away with, "Don't make such a fuss. I was tired of you clomping around in those shoes, disturbing my quiet." Ula vowed to be nicer to the bug-eyed nun. It was all she had to give her.

Weeks passed, filled with cookery and cleaning. The hefty Sister liked to remind Ula it was no surprise her husband had gone to sea. "He was probably desperate for a decent meal. You don't know how to do anything."

It was true. The only dish she could cook was shirred eggs and a hot dog casserole. The Sister's skill in stretching two cans of Spam to feed twenty was nearly Biblical and an art that Ula secretly didn't mind learning.

She ate by herself in the kitchen while the Sisters dined in the adjoining hall. Even though the nuns rarely spoke, she looked forward to mealtime. Sister Heavé muted her grumblings. To Ula, joining in the communal *clink* of forks against plates buffed the raw edges of being an outsider.

Cleaning was a different pain. She hated the incessant parade of dishes and tea cups. Her hands were red and peeling. She wore the same dress every day, rinsing it three times a week in the soap the Candidates made. Even Sister Heavé commented how frowzy it was becoming. Her other dress—her good dress—still had the sleeve ripped off. Sister Heavé ignored her request for fabric. Back home, the used clothes the Ladies Circle gave to charity were better than her dresses. She hated this poverty.

At night, silence pushed down with the three-story weight of the stones above. Bored, slipper-footed, and wrapped in a blanket, she crept up the stairs, peeking around corners. The first floor had nooks, closets, and a useless library that didn't contain any *McCalls* magazines or even a *Ladies Home Journal.*

The nuns went to bed with the appearance of the first stars, and they arose long before light streaked the morning sky. Night after night, watching her wristwatch, she explored until she decided to risk the second floor—the living quarters.

It required sneaking past several nuns' rooms to reach a communal area. She was getting better at moving like the Sisters who never made a sound, though how they did it with their wooden-soled shoes was a mystery. Ula wanted to lift a habit and peek underneath. She suspected they'd learned some hovering technique.

One narrow, off-shoot hallway lead to a well-organized broom closet. She was sure the buckets and brushes were the tools of the Candidates and used to glorify God by scrubbing floors and cleaning toilets. Opposite the closet was a tiny arched door, the kind usually seen beneath a stairwell. Opening it quietly, Ula had to bend over to enter. She found herself in a cozy room. A small stone table held a statue of the most approachable Virgin Mary she'd ever seen. The saint held her arms wide in a welcoming hug, her head cocked to one side as though listening.

Below the friendly Mary, on the floor, a girl sat, crying.

Ula stepped backward, clonking her head on the four-foot high doorframe. "Damn!"

The girl looked up.

"*Shh. Shh.* Sorry," Ula whispered, pausing long enough to ask, "You okay?"

The girl, who appeared to be the same age, stood, smudging tears from her face. Her eyes darted around the room as though an escape route would appear.

"I cry too. I understand," Ula said. "And I know you're supposed to confess every sin, but please don't report me. I'm in enough trouble everyday as it is. The Sister will make me carve toothpicks from twigs if she knows."

The young woman stood mutely in her gray cotton gown and night cap. Ula peeked out the door, checking for nuns, then hesitated. "Honestly, it's none of my business, but I don't see how you and the others take it. Criminy! Sister Heavé may be a pain in the bohunkus, but at least she lets it out."

"That's why she's down in the kitchen." The young woman's eyes widened. She covered her mouth with her hand.

Ula pulled the door closed. "You condemn *talkers* to the kitchen?" she whispered, moving nearer the girl. "What do you have against talking?"

"Silence adds simplicity and humility to obedience. We are better able to focus on given tasks without adding the signature of our own likes and dislikes."

"You say that like you memorized it."

"I'm not supposed to be speaking to you."

"I'm not supposed to be here. What is this room...a sanctuary?" The girl nodded. "I don't get it." Ula frowned. "Why can't we talk? God talked. Jesus talked. Even your blessed Mary chattered and sang a tune."

"That's what Sister Heavé says. I heard that years ago she declared if God had wanted silent creatures, He would have halted creation on the fifth day and never made man. But she is an honored and valuable part of the community. Rather than have her leave, she works in the kitchen where she can be 'contained.' Though we're not supposed to know that."

"Is Plumpy—that's what I call her, but not to her face—is she supposed to be *containing* me too?"

The girl coughed a laugh then covered her mouth. Giggles escaped in muffled snorts. Ula grimaced, waving *be quiet* with both hands.

"I'm sorry," the young woman whispered. "It's just such glorious relief. Sometimes the only life I have is inside my own head."

"Why don't you leave—go home?"

"I can't. It's...complicated."

"You're telling me." Ula lowered into a cross-legged sit on the prayer rug, facing Saint Mary. "I can't go home either."

"I'm Marina." The young woman sat beside her. "You're Ula—we all know that much. Is it true you're married?"

"First tell me if it's true that everybody's bald under their coifs?"

It was long into the night before the girls finished their revelations.

Psalm 126
Those Who Sow With Tears...

A few weeks later, Sister Heavé came to the doorway of Ula's small eating alcove. "You need to come to the dining room." Ula held her breath. Someone must've discovered her midnight forays into the crannies of the convent. She covered her bowl of rabbit soup with her napkin and trudged after the hefty nun. Fifteen pairs of eyes watched her enter and stand before them. There would have been more, but the remaining hands of the cloister were serving in soup lines.

Mother Radagunda arose, her fingertips still touching the table on either side of her plate. "We have prepared something for you." She spoke quietly then nodded at another nun and sat down.

Sister Wingretta came forward. To Ula, most of the nuns looked alike because she rarely interacted with any of them. When she watched them at Compline, all she could see was six inches of each face framed in a white coif under a formless bulk of black fabric. However, Sister Wingretta was memorable. Her black, horn-rimmed glasses flared at the hinges, making her thick eyebrows look like extended wings. Ula had cubbyholed the Sister as the Mother's henchman, the summoner who called the pig-headed to stand before the Boss Nun. During her midnight confabs with Marina, she'd learned that Sister Wingretta was actually the Mother's secretary and an instructor of the Novices. Even more surprising was that the girls liked this nun who was in need of a good eyebrow plucking.

"The Novices have created a gift." The Sister nodded at Marina who looked so different now in her mid-calf habit, thick stockings, and white veil. The girl held out a brown paper

64

package tied with twine. "The design, cutting and sewing of this dress is by the Novices. It has been blessed for service. May you wear it with God's peace."

Ula stared at the package then her own faded dress frayed at the cuffs, thinning at the elbows and seat. Had they been talking about her and decided to clothe her before she became naked? Was this the way they treated charity cases? Her father may be a religious curmudgeon, but he'd demanded the Ladies' group never hold up someone's poverty, "then swoop in like saviors, accepting accolades for putting a Band-Aid on a cavernous wallet."

Wrinkled with previous use, the brown paper crackled slightly as Ula took it. Unsure what to say, she nodded a stiff smile around the room, being sure not to look at Marina. The two young women had been meeting on Thursday nights, verbally exorcising their complaints and fears. Perhaps that hadn't been such a good idea.

Ula stepped back toward the safety of her eating alcove.

"You may open it." Sister Radagunda interrupted her retreat. "I'm sure all of us would like to share the loving handiwork of the Novices with you."

"Oh." Not wishing to push dishes out of the way, Ula balanced the package on her knee and pulled the string. The paper fell off to reveal a work dress of heavy black cotton. The cuffs of the three-quarter-length sleeves were bound in gray denim. In a last-ditch effort at style, they'd added a Peter Pan collar also in gray. As she held it up against her body, she saw they had embroidered Bible verses in various colors around the hem and cuffs. A bright red, rather large, *Psalm 126* covered the heart.

It was the ugliest dress Ula had ever seen.

An anticipatory silence filled the room.

"I don't know if I should speak," Ula said, "but I'm going to anyway." She didn't look at Mother Radagunda but noticed the others were. "Weeks ago I would have rolled my eyes because..." Her words stopped. Not a chair scraped the floor. Not a water glass lifted to anyone's lips. All waited silently, patiently. Ula listened for a moment. For some reason, the stillness didn't feel strange to her anymore. It was truly comforting to be allowed to collect her thoughts without pressure.

In a softer voice she started again. "A month ago I was younger. Stupider. I thought I should only wear what I saw in magazines. Now I'm thankful just to be clothed. Fashions and styles change, but when you're clothed by people who care...that lasts longer. Thank you." Ula scanned their faces.

Most smiled and gave her a nod when she caught their eyes. The Novices beamed.

"Well said." Sister Heavé rapped the table, contributing the only noise to the room.

From a silent hand signal, the Candidates began gathering dishes, taking them to the kitchen. Ula hurried to her room. For such uncomely clothing, she was amazed at how touched she was. It fit surprisingly well and was shorter than a habit, though it would have been nice if it were cinched at the waist to show off a bit of figure. Maybe she could add a belt.

She returned to the kitchen in her new frock. "Was it you? Did you tell them I needed a dress?" she asked as Sister Heavé plunged a stack of dishes into hot water.

"Just because you got to make a speech in there, doesn't mean you should be workin' your jaw now. Here, wash. If those girls had taken any longer to sew it up, you'd be naked. Now, finish up. Mother wants to see you."

"Thanks." Ula gave her a hug.

"Get off me. Your hands are wet." The plump Sister swatted her with a dishtowel.

An hour later Ula knocked at Mother Radagunda's arched office door. She winced. She'd made a four-knock, *rap-rap-rap-rap,* echoing through the stone-walled hallway rather than the quick, soft double-tap the nuns used.

Once inside, she was instructed to sit. A wooden stool faced the desk. Ula hated that stool. It meant she was in the hot seat again. "You've received a letter. Someone from your boarding house brought it over." The Mother held the envelope between two fingers, like it was a cigarette, displaying it, but not offering it. "You never said you'd run away from your family."

"You read it?" Ula stared.

"Sister Larrine reads all outgoing and incoming mail for those who have not taken their vows. It is our way of caring for the Candidates and Novices entrusted to us. Sister Larrine was a bit overzealous and extended her boundaries by reading your mail, but what she saw alarmed her, and I'm glad she brought it to me. It seems you left home under less than ideal conditions."

"I don't see how that's any of your business. And I can't believe you read my mail. Who's it from? Never mind." Ula shoved her hand forward. "I can see for myself."

The Sister's face changed; her stare hardened and smoldered. Ula's hand lowered, her words evaporating from her mouth.

"You are wedded now, although it seems your husband cannot take care of you, appropriately." The Mother looked at nothing and everything on her desk. "I suppose what's done is done, and we ask God's grace in making the best of it. But I believe your mother has every right to be concerned. You will write to your parents immediately, telling them where you are and your state of affairs. You will speak truthfully and frankly. I will include a letter to them also. I expect your missive on my desk before Compline tomorrow."

"Sister Larrine is going to read my outgoing mail too?"

"No." The nun's icy stare said this was the end of the discussion. "I will read it."

"I don't have pen and paper—or money to buy them," Ula said quietly, "or I would've written before now. I can't write my husband. He's not allowed to say where he is."

The hard lines of the nun's face melded into weariness as she let out an exasperated breath. "We would've gladly provided pen and paper had you asked. But since this is the barrier which keeps you from communicating, you will solve it by your means rather than ours. You have earned a small stipend for the work you've done. I'll give some of it to Sister Heavé. You'll accompany her and assist in the soup lines tomorrow. Afterward, she will help you purchase what you need."

Ula's fists clenched at her sides as she chanced a white-hot glance at the Mother. She'd worked harder than she ever had at home. She followed their rules—most of them. She deserved to be treated like an adult, not ordered about like one of their blank-faced girls murmuring, "Yes, Sister. Thank you, Sister. Please kick me when I'm down, Sister." Her lips tightened over her mouth, holding back words while a different thought stabbed her conscience.

Holy piglucky! This would be a chance to get out for a while. See the town. Talk with people who didn't wear three yards of fabric wrapped around their skulls. Maybe this was supposed to be penance, but it didn't have to be.

Ducking her head, she gave an obligatory nod and walked out without waiting to be dismissed, unaware the price of a snide attitude would always be paid.

The next day, Ula helped Sister Heavé in every way possible. She carried pots. Stood where she was told to stand and was quick to obey. When folks began coming through the line, she machine-gunned them with friendly questions. "Do you like this weather? Where ya from? How long you been here? How are you feeling? Do you have any kids?"

Sister Heavé stared with her hands on her hips, "Have you swallowed a bunch of people, and they're all trying to talk at once?"

By two o'clock the noise of the lunchroom throbbed in Ula's head. Wooden folding chairs scraped across the linoleum. A constant hum of voices fogged the room. Silverware clattered in dishpans. Metal kettles banged in the sink. "It can be overwhelming when you're used to the quiet." The Sister set down a tray of clinking glassware. "Of course, all that yammering you were doing earlier didn't help."

By the time they reached the dime store, Ula felt crosseyed. She rubbed her temples, leaving Sister Heavé to muse over the paper selection.

"I think your mister would like this. And maybe this for your mom. A little color, but not too fancy."

"I don't give a damn. Pick out something and let's go home."

"I'd have thought your sore knees and raw hands from scrubbing floors would've taught you to mind your tongue, but I guess not. Your dirty mouth just earned you toilet-cleaning for a week. I'm sorry about your headache, but it's no excuse to be profane. Now which of these papers do you like? Stationary says as much about the person as the words on the paper."

"Then pick out something penitent and I'll send blank sheets."

The Sister's face became a thundercloud, but she waited until they got on the street car before unleashing her harangue. "You are an ungrateful upstart. Mark my words, your uncaring heart will leave you nothing but a future of loneliness. That dress you're wearing. Do you know what any of the Bible verses say? No? The Novices were told to contemplate God's will and pray for appropriate scripture all the while they cut and stitched. Each text was put upon their heart for your guidance.

It really *is* a special garment. Aren't you even curious enough to look up the verses?"

"Oh hooray. Now I have a dress that gives me homework," Ula groaned.

The two women weren't speaking by the time they reached the doors of The Holy Trail.

Sister Wingretta met them in the entry, her eyes wide behind her horn-rim glasses. "Ula is excused from supper preparations."

"Whatever for?" Sister Heavé scowled, waiting for more.

A burst of laughter came from Mother Radagunda's office, echoing down the hallway. The plump nun's eyebrows shot up. Her forehead furrowed. Sister Wingretta took Ula by the arm, guiding her to the office. Uninvited, Sister Heavé followed.

They paused before they reached the door. "What in St. Peter's name—?" Sister Heavé started.

Sister Wingretta held up her hand, shaking her head. "I cannot say." She waved Ula in, but Ula didn't budge. She'd learned that lesson in the sixth grade when a raccoon had gotten into Patty's house. Never go through a door that others were unwilling to enter.

That's when Sister Wingretta gave Ula a push.

Cherry Grapefruit Pudding

*U*la stumbled into the office, surprised to see a large brown growler of beer and six bottles of Coca-Cola on the Mother's desk. The nun looked up, the lingering hint of laughter still on her face. Kol hitched his arm slightly over the back of the chair, turning to see who was behind him.

Ula stood dumbfounded. She'd been here weeks and had rarely heard laughter. If she did, it was a muffled giggle from a Candidate or Novice. And here sat the Mother and Kol wittering like old chums. He even rated the good chair, not that damn stool she had to sit on for inquisitions. Ula looked around for the devil seat and saw it in the corner of the room.

"Well, go on," Sister Heavé called, "Grab him."

Ula's shoes felt nailed to the floor. She turned to see the hefty nun and Sister Wingretta peeking from the doorway. Obviously, nothing was private, even in a convent. "I...I..." Before she could form more words, Kol had crossed the room. Her trapped arms waved uselessly as he gave her a hug. He kissed the top of her head mumbling, "I'm glad you found your way here. I'm so sorry you were afraid."

Ula squirmed to free an arm, feeling like she was five years old at the grocery store again. She'd sneaked away from her mother's cart and lay on top of big bags of dog food beneath a shelf. From her hiding spot, she spied on feet walking by and eavesdropped on conversations. When her mother had finally found her, she was hugged and berated at the same time. Ula had felt both sad and relieved. Her secret freedom was over, but at least she was special enough to be searched for, not abandoned.

Mother Radagunda arose. "Sisters, this is Captain Kol Kellner of the Merchant Marine, Ula's husband." She gave a single you-may-enter wave to the nuns in the doorway. "And...he comes bearing gifts." She pointed at the growler and sodas.

"Would you be Roman Catholic?" Sister Heavé eyed the crockery jug of beer.

"Norwegian Lutheran. But I've heard that German nuns don't mind a good beer. I had an aunt who took her vows."

"That's close enough. I'm Sister Heavé." She hefted the growler off the desk and gave Kol's hand a single shake. "And this is Sister Wingretta." The other Sister gave him a shy smile before focusing on the floor.

"Captain Kellner?" Mother walked from behind the desk. "We don't wish to intrude on your personal respite with your wife tonight, but tomorrow, if it wouldn't be too much of an imposition, could you spare a half hour to tell us how the war is going? We don't have a radio. We'd greatly appreciate any news you could share. Each of us has a relative or friend we're worried about. The papers say it's going better, but any news you could share would be helpful to our community of Sisters."

"I'll tell you what I can."

"Tomorrow at two?" The Mother wasn't asking him; she was looking at Sister Heavé, who nodded that she could cook something up.

"Now, before Ula leaves..." the Mother's smile turned official, "she has promised to write a letter to her father, informing him of her new address and the present state of affairs."

"You can't be serious." Ula's face had a slack-jawed stare. "Now?"

"I am." Her smile hardened into the look she wore for stiff-necked sinners. "It's long overdue, and previously you agreed it would be done by Compline."

Kol touched her arm. "It'll only take a minute if you hop to."

Ignoring the daggered look Ula was shooting at her husband, Sister Heavé offered, "I'm sure I can find a sandwich, Captain, while your missus writes her family."

"I wouldn't want to make work for you, Sister, but if you had a leftover biscuit, I wouldn't say no."

"I've got a bit of blackberry jam too." Sister Heave´ patted the jug then grabbed Ula, ushering her to the door. "We might even find a spot of butter."

"But I have a headache." Ula's whine reverberated through the study.

The stout sister gave Ula a little nudge out of the room. "I'm sure I have some powders for that." She beckoned for Kol to follow his wife.

"By your leave," the Captain said to Mother Radgunda and received her nod before stepping into the hallway.

Sister Heavé paused at the door, exchanging a serious look with the Mother. The head nun arched an eyebrow, and then sat down to her duties, shaking her head.

In the kitchen, Ula dumped bitter aspirin powder onto her tongue then gulped a glass of water. Tearing a blank page from the grocery notepad, she stood at the chopping block, scribbling a message.

"No. No. No. Shoo!" The chunky Sister slapped the new box of stationary on top of her writing. "You can't find the right words when you're thinking about everything but what you're doing. Go to your room and write a proper letter."

Kol gave Ula a conspiratorial wink. "I'm sure you'll be done before the next bell. Go. I'll wait."

Ula was angry enough to spit in the communion chalice. Refusing to cooperate completely, she moved only as far as the eating alcove, listening to Sister Heavé dote on Kol like he was a long-lost son.

She dashed off the letter, purposely absent of emotion, punching the periods hard enough to pierce the paper. *Hello Mother and Father. I am fine. I stay at a convent when Kol is at sea. You may write me here. The address is on the envelope. All is well. Don't worry. I haven't converted. Ula.*

From her late night conclaves with Marina, Ula knew better than to cast shadows on the nuns. She'd heard the Novice's stories of sitting on stone floors to eat meals, or asking for-giveness for walking too fast, or confessing to dropping a hairbrush and disturbing the Grand Silence. Sister Plumpy would insist on a hundred rewrites if anything was mentioned about the strangling obedience the nuns drilled into their captives.

"Here. Done." Ula shoved the folded paper at the Sister, and then rolled her eyes when she was told to take it to the Mother.

She marched upstairs, stomping on each step so it echoed through the halls, enjoying the dent it put in the nuns' silence.

Mother Radagunda read the ivory-colored sheet and lay it down, frowning. "It seems rather terse for a young woman so far from her family." She watched Ula's eyes empty as the girl gave a one-shouldered shrug. "Very well then," the Mother continued. "I will fill the gaps with a letter of my own." Her voice was underlined with threat, but it was lost on her audi-ence. The young woman in front of her stared at the air. Her face held the same blank look of the Novices. The Mother sighed. It would be good for this girl to be away for several days. She'd already been around the community long enough to master the art of concealing who she really was beneath.

The Mother gave a sad nod. "We'll see you and the Captain at tea tomorrow."

***

"I don't get to eat with them—not that I want to because they never say anything." Ula paced the small room. "They don't even pray out loud. The place is about as lively as watching water freeze. And then *you* waltz in and it's...'Oooooh. Let's have tea with the Captain.'" She batted his hand away from the buttons at the front of her Bible dress. "'Oooooh, how's the war going, Captain? What do you and Roosevelt have planned next, sir?'"

Kol let out a long breath then began chuckling. They had returned to the boarding house, but discovered the landlord had sublet Ula's room and was collecting double rent. She'd stopped Kol from breaking the landlord's arm, by whacking the guy on his bald head with a newspaper, shouting "I've got a headache, just give us a room and fix the problem."

Now they were staying in a bedroom in the landlord's personal quarters. She'd changed. The Ula he'd brought from Oklahoma would've been crying by now. This Ula threw her hands in the air and ranted. At least she didn't cuss anymore, not like she had when she was staying here, eavesdropping on the pipefitters. He wondered if the nuns had soaped her mouth.

"But you," she continued. "You walk into a convent with sodas and beer, and you're cooler than Frank Sinatra."

Lord, but she was beautiful. He was surprised how often she'd come to mind each day. He'd made mental notes of things he wanted to show her. The Milky Way on a black night. Early mornings when the ocean was fiery-pink and smooth as glass. The smell of land carried by the wind after they'd been at sea for days. She'd appreciate the beauty. She wasn't like other girls, talking nail polish and Hedy Lamarr's hairstyle. She was genuine and honest. And a pain in the butt. "Sit down. Let me take care of that headache." He patted the bed.

She plunked beside him. He squeezed her shoulders in a deep massage. "Happy Birthday. Sorry, my hands are rough. Ropes and saltwater."

"Today's my birthday?" She gaped at Kol.

"Last week. Sorry I didn't make it on time."

Ula turned, her slouch growing even more hump-backed. "I didn't even know. This is ungodly sad and maddening. I've got to get out of that infernal convent. I haven't seen a calendar in..." She let out a satisfied groan as he worked a knot out of her neck. "And why does everyone like you?" She sighed. "Even Mother Radagunda—that's like capturing Monte Cassino."

"Look who's keeping up with the war. Can you still tell me who's on the Pop chart this week?"

"I haven't heard music that isn't a hymn or liturgical chant in weeks. And I served in the soup lines today. The Cassino battle was all everyone was talking about—not my birthday, if you can believe that."

"Good for you. Well, my charm is easily explained. Besides being a loveable guy, I've had experience with convents. We always took treats when we visited Aunt Chloe. She let us kids call her that. Adults had to call her Sister Gregory. When I'd read where you'd gone, I headed for a bar." He kissed the soft crook in her neck.

Her shoulders slumped; her eyes closed. The warmth of his breath traveled up her spine as she leaned into him. "They think you're the cat's meow. Sister Radagunda will probably make me write to you every day and read the letters to make sure I do."

"Would that be so bad?" His lips worked his way up her neck.

"And where would I send them?" She leaned away. "You left me sitting in a pighole without a clue where you'd gone or if you'd return."

"Ula, it takes months for letters to find me—if the mail ship isn't torpedoed. Often I don't know where I'm going. I get orders at sea. What do you want of me?" He flopped back on the bed.

"I want to be responsible for my own place. I thought I'd be fixing up a home for you to come back to, and I'd have other war wives to do things with. Instead, I'm either scared stiff on skid-row, or I'm treated like a ten-year-old, living in the basement of a convent. It's not supposed to be like this. I want to spend tomorrow, finding another place to live."

They were quiet for a moment, staring at each other.

"Ula...you'll need to go back to Holy Trail."

"What? No."

"Or go home."

"Why?"

"Because I've been transferred from a coaster to a Liberty ship. I won't be running supplies through the canal to the east coast anymore. They need Mariners to haul troops and cargo across the Pacific. The trips will be longer—three to six months. If you were in a different boarding house, you'd still be alone. In the convent there are people to look after you—"

"I don't want to be *looked after*. I want to be responsible for myself and be treated like an adult."

"You're in a community at the nunnery," Kol continued. "I need you to stay there, or go home so I don't worry."

"I'm not going home."

"I figured. So I talked to Mother Radagunda—" He held up a hand, stifling her complaints. "I offered to pay your room and board, but she said you worked for that. There was a small stipend which you'd earned. I gave it all back to them."

"You what?" Ula sat up on her knees, boring a hole in him with her stare. "You had no right. It's mine. I earned it. I need it for...for... . Look, they've got some repellant ideas about...a woman's hygiene." She couldn't bear to tell him about hand washing menstrual pads made of flannel.

"I told them it was my job to support you, not theirs."

"Well, where's your support? I have one rag of a dress. One with a missing sleeve. And this walking Bible study." She flounced the black skirt. "Mother Radagunda doles out my stipend in miserly bits and doesn't even trust me with it. She gave it to Sister Plumpy to buy stationary. They treat me like a little kid."

"They treat you like you act."

The silence lasted a long, hurtful moment. Then Ula pierced it with a rant.

For a woman with a headache and a man who had been at sea, the following hours of words were a waste of precious time. It was long into the morning before the bed springs creaked.

Sister Heavé hefted a tea kettle from the stove and poured a little hot water into two ceramic tea pots. "You'll be proud of the missus. She's learned to cook since she came here." The Sister handed Kol a broken piece of gingersnap. "Lord help us, we were hungry when she first started cooking. She used to burn everything she tried."

"I did not." Ula unmolded small chilled tins of Cherry-Grapefruit Pudding. "You'd better appreciate this, Kol." She placed a gingersnap beside each jiggly mound. "Not even the Vicar gets cookies. And one of the nuns stood in a food line for an hour to get the corn syrup that went into these. When this war is over, I'm going to eat as much dessert as I want."

"Well, you won't starve on her cooking when the war's over, Captain; we'll make sure of that." The Sister sloshed the hot water around, warming the pots, and then dumped it out. "The missus is going to try handwork next. Every woman needs to sew and knit."

"My mother taught me to stitch," Ula said, watching the Sister mouth a silent *Pffft*. "I can't right now because I don't have any material." She gave the Sister a sharp look. "I can't even get a scrap to make a sleeve for my dress. I suppose I could take the rags from the mop and weave something together."

"Good idea! Use it up, wear it out, make it do. Until then, I'll light a candle for you, *dummchen*."

"What is that? Do you know?" Ula asked Kol who was wiping a smile from his face. He glanced at the nun.

The Sister filled the pots with steaming water. "It means dolly." She glanced toward Kol, who quickly looked away, apparently aware that it also meant ding-a-ling.

"See!" Ula arranged a broken cookie next to a pudding. "This is what I put up with day after day. I'm with one of the few nuns who doesn't believe in silence, and she uses all of her unholy chatter on me."

Kol quickly stood. "Let me carry those pots for you, Sister." He grabbed the tray before the pudgy nun had snugged the cozies over them.

"Oh, no." She pushed his hand away. "That wouldn't be right. Ula can do it."

Ula leveled a glare at him.

Kol was surprised to find twenty women seated and quietly waiting. After Mother Radagunda's introduction, he swallowed and began.

"I'm sure most of you know that during peacetime, the ships known as the Merchant Marine carry imports and exports throughout the world, but during war that role changes. The fleet is nationalized, meaning it becomes naval auxiliary. If you have a friend or relative overseas, there's a good chance the Merchant Marine carried them there. The U.S. government now controls all of our cargo and fleet movement. They put heavy artillery along with Navy gunners on each ship to help our men and supplies reach their destination. Where the Navy goes, the Merchant Marine is there too. Usually in groups but sometimes a ship has to travel solo." He looked at their faces.

These women didn't need to know about the cold sweats to make port or picking up survivors by the light of a burning vessel. They, like the rest of the world, needed to believe the same weekly newspaper report: Two Allied ships sunk in the Atlantic. In reality, it was thirty-three. The dashing stories men told in bars about evading subs, mines, and kamikaze pilots didn't belong here.

"Because so many of our losses occur at night, I'm asking you to tell your friends and relatives to honor the blackouts. Use your window shades, cover the headlights on cars. The enemy's off-shore subs use the city's lights to see the silhouettes of our ships working along the coast. You can save thousands of lives by hiding your lights.

"I'm not sure what you're interested in. I don't know about the ground battles. And I can't say where I take troops or supplies, but you know that. Why don't you ask me questions?"

Several nuns had notes ready which they passed to Mother Radagunda, who read them and selected questions. "Are our men hungry?' Are they getting supplies? Is there enough in the Red Cross packages? Is it true Japan won't give Red Cross packages to prisoners of war?" As more notes were passed to the Mother, Kol sensed what was on these women's hearts. They'd heard the patriotic chatter from Fireside Chats and ration-line rumors. They were desperate to peel away propaganda and know if their loved ones were all right.

Kol answered, trying for the truth, attempting to leave threads of hope. Until he reached a question that brought back too many images of grown men crying.

"Are the men afraid?"

He looked down. The nuns waited. Silence blanketed the room. He rubbed his hand over his mouth then looked up. "Yes, sometimes. Oh...there's laughing, and poker, and showing off pin-up girls. But the nearer we get to the destination, the quieter it gets. Night time is the hardest. Maybe it's the blackness all around. A lot of prayers go up at night.

"And then all their training kicks in. They do what they've practiced. They don't think about it. They do what they have to do. Will it be over soon? I wish I knew. We've had important victories in Stalingrad and Sicily. I can tell you this. Your prayers are important. Every little thing from saving grease to doing without sugar is more important than you know. And please, don't ever stop praying for us."

Ula wanted to applaud. That was her husband up there. The Navy may not take him because of missing fingers, but he was still Captain of a ship, trying to stop Yamamoto from overrunning the Pacific.

There was no applause. Mother Radagunda stood and led them in prayer.

Kol left that evening, but not without another row. He'd send Ula a monthly check, but it would be small. Mostly because she didn't need a lot at the convent. Secondly, she shouldn't be buying much. New dresses, magazines, or sweets would only cause a rift between her and the stripped-down lifestyle of the nuns. And lastly, her "spending money" was small because he was saving for a boat. "The war won't go on forever. This is my chance to be my own boss and make a living in the years to come."

Ula argued, but even she could hear how silly she sounded campaigning for furniture and a house right now. She consoled herself with the two chocolate bars and a pack of gum he'd given her. "I'll have to hide these." She'd hugged the chocolate to her chest. "Sister Snoop—I don't know her name. She doesn't talk to me, but she goes through my mail and the other girls' letters and packages, taking gifts—even underwear. She misers it away, and when she finally doles out candy or cake, it goes to everyone. It's usually hard and dried up by then. Sharing is a big deal with these nuns."

"Imagine that," Kol replied.

The following week, two packages arrived. One was a bolt of black, heavy-duty cloth—suitable for habits. The other was three yards of a pink floral print.

Ula would have never known of its arrival if Sister Heavé hadn't placed the soft material on a chair next to her while she was making kidney stew.

"We can't use this, but you might. And there's also enough for five habits. God be praised. We were wondering how we would take care of the Novices ready to take their vows. How your Captain got his hands on this, I don't want to know."

"Did he send thread?" Ula shook out the floral print to check width and length.

"Don't be asking for everything. Besides, he's a man. What would he know about hems and hooks?" The Sister pulled the fabric from Ula's hands. "You'll learn how to knit a scarf first. Those winds blow cold across a ship's deck. After lunch you can write a letter thanking your mister."

Ula whacked harder at the veal kidneys on the chopping block. She clenched her teeth, holding back words or Plumpy might demand she shear a sheep and spin the wool before making her learn to knit. By the time she'd punished an onion into minced bits, she'd calmed enough to ask, "How much will the yarn cost?"

"Oh." Sister paused, ladling a spoonful of lard into an iron skillet. Her eyes scanned her mental files. "There's no wool with the war on. I know of an old sweater you can unravel and use. You can borrow my needles until you can afford your own."

Ula quickly turned to hide her face. The Sister didn't know Kol had given her money before he left. It wasn't much, but it was one precious tidbit the nuns didn't know. "Thank you." Her voice carried a smile.

They had their fingers in all the nooks and crannies of her life. They were aware that she and Kol had eloped. They knew the rough start of her marriage. They controlled what she ate, read, and bought. It was like living at home. But here was one thing they didn't know. Oh, they'd find out next month when Sister Snoop would dutifully report Kol had sent her a check. But they didn't know about her tiny stash of cash and chocolate bars. She was going to have to find a better place than her pillow case to hide them.

She felt glee at having one secret all to herself. She had better things to buy than yarn. She was saving for a pair of peep-toe, platform, slingback shoes.

Where Did You Go?

W orking with yarn and needles was like weaving spaghetti with an icepick. Ula didn't have the patience to sit still, wrapping yarn around sticks, much less count the loopy mess.

It was becoming questionable whether Sister Heavé had the patience either. "How did you do this?" The nun pulled at stitches until the yarn snagged to a stop. "I've never seen a nest like this. I knew a Sister who had arthritis so bad she couldn't use her hands. She learned to knit with her feet. I tell you, her lop-sided potholders were better than this rat's bumble."

"Why don't we start with something I can do and make a dress?"

"Uh-uh-uh, Cinderella. There'll be no sewing until there's a scarf for the mister."

"I'm going to write to Tommy while you cuss under your breath."

"I do not curse. Though if ever there were a sanctioned reason to swear, this would qualify." The Sister used the point of a needle to work a lump of yarn loose. "Bring your paper in here. You can write at the table. I'm not working on these Boy Scout knots alone. And pick up your feet."

Ula let out a loud sigh and continued shuffling to her room. She was eighteen years old, married, and treated like a baby. Actually she'd turned seventeen, but she'd told the nuns eighteen, and she was sticking to it.

"That's the boy from your home town, isn't it? Infantry somewhere in Europe?"

"Does Sister Snoop have to read everything and tell you about it?" Ula called as she tromped back upstairs and slapped her stationary on the table. "It's a boy I went to school with. I write to him and my brother, Joe, to keep their spirits up. Tommy doesn't have any family. My letters are probably the only ones he gets. Is that all right with you?"

Sister Heavé blinked. "No need to get snippy. I think it's nice. I was just making conversation."

Quietness settled over the kitchen with only the sound of Ula's pen scritching ink on the paper. The Sister picked at the yarn. After a moment, her question rushed out as though it had been trapped behind a dam. "He's the one who had bombs dropping around him until he had ringing in his ears, isn't he? I think he's in that terrible mess in Anzio."

"Why don't *you* write him instead?"

"Tell him we're praying for him." The Sister pressed the wooly beginnings of a scarf flat on the table. "There. You can start torturing this yarn again after lunch."

Two days later, a V-Mail lay on Ula's bed. The small 2 x 3 inch envelope was from Tommy. It could wait until after supper. She checked the backside. It had been opened. Sister Heavé would probably tell her all about it.

The plump Sister was preoccupied, fussing over soya beans, peeling the pork rind off the top of the pot, and complaining that after six hours of baking, "the little devils" still weren't done. Heroic efforts to crank up the old eight-burner stove and cook them faster didn't work. They had to make an emergency Peanut Bisque soup, and still, supper was late.

Ula fell onto her narrow bed, exhausted. She pulled the tiny photocopied sheet from Tommy's envelope and found it heavily redacted with cut-out slits. The handwriting was rough, as though it had been scribbled while doing jumping jacks. He described the heavy fighting, bombs exploding, and men screaming. "I spend every night, hiding in the black bottom of a foxhole, crying. I can't stop shaking."

She read the letter again, becoming even more disgusted the second time. What a coward. He'd always been quiet and timid in high school, but this was too much. Granted, the battle was terrible, but what if her brother or Kol cried every time they felt threatened? We'd be shouting *Heil Hitler* right now instead of listening to Fireside chats.

She ripped the letter in half and threw it in the trash. She'd never write to the little mouse again.

Sister Wingretta appeared in the kitchen on a Tuesday afternoon and beckoned. Ula gladly dropped the burnt pot she was scrubbing, peeled off her apron, and followed. The nun slowed, in order to walk beside Ula. "It was very kind of your husband to reassure us. My brother is on the *John Barry*. I keep thinking of Mrs. Sullivan. All five sons lost when the *Juneau* was torpedoed, and survivors left in the ocean for eight days. My brother can't swim. I can't... ." She stopped walking and hung her head, trying to collect herself.

Ula stared. This nun rarely spoke to her and had never said anything so personal. She touched the Sister's arm. "Pray?" The nun had barely nodded before Ula whispered, "Lord, Be with our men. Save us from our fears. Amen."

The Sister looked up, pain and curiosity in her eyes. Ula patted the nun's arm. She may have just proven she wasn't a God-hating heathen, but she still wasn't going to say anything in Compline. Or maybe the Sister's look was for the rough little prayer. Not eloquent like the ones the nuns sang. It was enough.

Ula turned and started walking. Her father would be proud to hear a Catholic and a Lutheran praying together again. It had only taken a war to achieve it.

The thought startled her. Why should she care a whit what her father thought?

Mother Radagunda waved for Ula to enter when she double-tapped the open door. "Please sit." Ula noted it was an upholstered chair. "Sister Heavé reports that you're learning and performing duties well. We feel that you may be entrusted with more responsibility. You may assist with the paper drives and help with the shopping. Would you be willing to do that?"

"Yes, Mother." She hoped she hadn't sounded too excited. She wanted her tone to be quiet and subservient. The same way she'd heard nuns say it a hundred times a day.

"Because you are a married woman, we feel your correspondence should be private. Your mail will not be read." She handed Ula an envelope.

The "E" on Eulalia was looped with flourishes. Her mother's penmanship. She flipped the envelope over. Still sealed. "So...now that you've met Kol, I'm treated differently?"

"You understand that you appeared to us bloodied, with a suitcase, and in despair. There was some doubt as to the authenticity of your story. It was for your protection as well as that of our community of Sisters."

Ula opened her mouth then thought better of it. "I understand, Mother." She nodded. When dismissed, she stepped into the hallway and ripped open the letter. If she read it in the kitchen, Sister Heavé would pester her for every word.

Her shriek echoed through the corridor, bringing Sister Wingretta from her cubby-hole office next to Mother's study.

Ula shoved the white envelope into the Sister's hands. For a brief moment it seemed odd that the first private letter she'd received, she'd given back to the nuns to read. The thought lasted less than a second as she collapsed against the Sister in tears.

***

"I know you're not Roman Catholic, but I don't think you'll break Luther's precious theology by lighting a candle for your brother." Sister Heavé guided Ula's hand to a wick.

Ula numbly allowed being handled. Light. That was a good thing, wasn't it? Maybe it would push back the blackness so she could breathe.

She sat at the back of the chapel, silent as usual. Tonight she had an unending stream of tears. Though most of the nuns rarely spoke, they all sang. High clear voices, thanking God, asking him to watch over the world as it slept.

She wondered if Joe slept eternally or just for the night? Her mother's letter said his B-25 went down in a raid on oil fields in Turkey. It had happened three weeks ago. Surely if he were dead, they'd know by now. Missing in action hopefully meant he was in a prison camp.

Afterward, Sister Wingretta took Ula's arm, leading her to the Great Room. Ula had laughed at the name when she'd first arrived. It wasn't great at all. Filled with mismatched, over-stuffed, cast-off chairs, it was a small room where the nuns gathered after dinner to read or talk before the Grand Silence began.

Sister Heavé put a pieced-together quilt square in Ula's hand. "Embroider a few stitches over the seams," she whispered. "I know you know how to do that." The stout nun plopped on one side of Ula, sinking low in the couch, and started knitting a baby's cap. Sister Wingretta sat on the other side, a shuttle and cream-colored thread in her hands.

One by one, the nuns entered with their projects. Two Novices came to the door, whispering to the nearest nun. With a nod of the nun's black-veiled head, the Novices were allowed inside, sitting in folding chairs at the edge of the room. Marina caught Ula's eyes before turning them to focus on the collar of the habit she was sewing.

Ula looked around the room. These women—she didn't even know many of their names—sat with her. There were no words. Occasionally someone shifted in her chair, needles clicked together, a scissor snipped a thread.

One of Ula's tears splatted her fabric, a dark circle growing on the material. A hand appeared with a hankie. She didn't look up. Ula wasn't sure if she was crying over Joe. Maybe it was for Tommy. Perhaps it was the overwhelming sacredness within the silence. Without words, she felt the quiet support of women holding her up. Suffering with her. Praying for her. A bandage of the purest intent, damping the seeping edges of her wound. There was no need for words.

Sister Heavé watched Ula through the window. It should have taken ten minutes to sweep the inner courtyard, but Ula had been at it for a half hour. The nun had hoped that the rare appearance of February sunshine would perk the girl up. Instead, Ula pushed a leaf in one direction, then the other. "If this is how she worries for her brother, heaven help us if the Captain dies," the Sister muttered to herself and opened the door. "C'mon, we've got shopping to do. Shake a leg."

Without a word, Ula trudged inside, dragging the broom behind her.

She seemed to liven up on the street car, watching the people around her. Before they got off, they could see the line in front of Todd's Market. The late afternoon sun cast long shadows into the street.

"I should've known," Sister Heavé growled. "The milk lady blabbed about Todd getting ham shanks."

They took their place in the block-long queue behind two well-dressed women. One wore a high-cuffed pea-green hat with matching pumps and purse. The other had a wide, swoopy hat and gored skirt. Both women glanced to see who stood behind them then returned to their gossip.

"I need for you to stay in this line. I'm going over to the…" Sister Heavé looked around, lowering her voice, "the A&P. I heard they had *fresh apples*." She mouthed the two words. "I'd like to make a pie with something besides sweet taters. You hear me?"

Ula gave her a dull look. Who cared? Any pie would be better than what Joe or the boys at the front were eating—if they were alive.

She felt a little shake. "Listen to me," the Sister was saying. "Try to get at least three pounds. More if you can. Do not lose these ration stamps." The Sister tucked booklets into Ula's pocket. "You hear me?"

Ula nodded.

"Say it back."

"Get all I can get." Ula patted her left sweater pocket. "Of…" Her words stalled.

"Of ham! Mother Mary preserve us! Just stand here. Hold our place. I'll try to be back before you get to the store." She turned and trotted off.

Ula watched an empty package of Lucky Strikes dance across the street, blown and bounced by passing cars. People hurried by. Even the shoppers waiting in line seemed busy, smoking, chatting, or reading the paper. Everyone moved with purpose—except her.

"And then they eloped."

"Nooooooo," the swoopy-hatted lady in front of Ula gasped.

"Yeeeeees!" The other woman had a knowing look, spreading her gloved hand to make five pea-green exclamation points to her statement. "Well, it's not surprising. I've always said there were skeletons in that family's closet. There's something wrong with the parents if the kids run off and elope."

"What?" Ula squinted.

Mrs. Pea-Green turned, scrutinizing Ula from the hem of her black, verse-embroidered dress to her work-ready hairstyle, tied back like a Candidate's. The other woman wore a frosty glare. Ula ignored it; she'd learned the new etiquette of wartime: There were no private conversations. "That's not true," she said. "People elope all the time anymore. Decent people. There's no difference between eloping and a church wedding— except saving a lot of money."

"And breaking parents' hearts." The woman closed her eyes. The feather on her pea-green hat quivered as she shook her head. "In this case, it's worse. They just eloped. They never went to a Justice of the Peace."

"So?"

Mrs. Pea-Green's eyes flashed open. "They're living in sin! They can't call it marriage. It's not legal. It's...shacking up."

"Wait a minute." Ula grabbed the woman's arm, a frown scouring her face. "I've heard church ladies say a girl eloped instead of having a church wedding. It's the same thing."

"It most certainly *is* not." Mrs. Swoopy-Hat put her hand to her chest. "What do they teach at those Catholic schools?"

"I'm not Catholic. And magazines are full of celebrities who elope. You're telling me they're not really married if it's not in a church?"

"No. I'm saying if they don't use a clergyman, then they'd better stop at the Justice of the Peace. There are licenses to fill out and forms to sign. Where did you get married?" Mrs. Pea-Green pointed to Ula's ring.

Ula's hand dropped from the woman's arm, her mind replaying the September night with Kol. He'd put her suitcase in the back seat, asking silly questions. *Was she sure? Did she know how hard it was going to be?* "Yes, yes. yes. Let's just go." She'd wanted to get out of there before her dad woke up and the porch light came on. Kol had slipped his mother's ring on her finger. "This will have to do until there's time to do better." Ula had thought they'd never get beyond the driveway. She kept peering over the back seat, checking for lights, as they drove away.

Mrs. Pea-Green repeated her question, "Where were you married?"

"Oklahoma," Ula mumbled still watching her mental movie fade to black.

The two women gave each other *that-explains-everything* looks. Mrs. Swoopy-Hat's voice became casual, as though discussing dental cream. "Was it a church wedding or...Justice of the Peace?"

Ula looked up. If those were her only two options, and she hadn't taken either one of them then.... She swallowed. "My father is a Lutheran minister."

"Oh!" Both ladies laughed and relaxed. "No wonder you don't know anything about eloping. You church girls are so protected. Everyone in the congregation probably helped with your wedding. I hope you had some say in what you wanted."

Ula nodded, staring at nothing, her thoughts far away in Ponca City. "I probably...should've talked to my mother more."

"Exactly." Mrs. Pea-Green pointed her finger at her friend. "See? That's just what I was saying. There's something wrong with the parents and their communication if a kid runs away and elopes. Young people think the war has changed all the rules, but it's no excuse to live in sin." She shot a confirming nod toward Ula.

Ula wasn't there.

"Hey! Slow down!" a man yelled. Ula kept running, bumping into people, stumbling over curbs, crossing streets wherever the traffic light was green. The sour taste of panic bloomed in her throat and filled her mouth. She needed to get away, far away. There was something nauseating and ugly in the woman's words. A bell clanged wildly. A street car passed within inches. The conductor yelled. Ula stalled in the middle of the street.

"Whoa, girl! You gonna get yourself killed," a woman shouted. "Get over here. Big bus is comin' and you'll be wearin' it next thing you know."

A car honked. Ula winced, backing up. "Get your skinny little butt over here right now." Another woman ordered, and then both women began yelling at her. Ula dumbly followed their voices like a lifeline towing her out of deep water. She stepped onto the curb in a daze.

"It's shift change. They'd run over Franklin Delano if he stood between them and their beer." Two black women sat on the curb, watching her. Heavy leather boots stuck out from their cuffed jeans. Their flannel-shirted elbows rested on their knees. One had her hair tied in a blue bandana. Dented metal boxes sat beside them.

"I...I...." Ula looked around.

"You look lost—in more ways than one. Sit down here. Why you playing tag with the street car?"

"I..." Ula put a hand to her face. "I thought I was married, but—"

"I knew it!" The woman in the bandana shouted. "Only a man makes you crazy 'nuff to dance with cars."

"Hush up, Lee, let 'er talk. You go ahead, honey."

"He...took me away...from my home. But a woman in the grocery line told me that eloping doesn't mean you're married."

"No, baby. It don't." Both women shook their heads. "Uh-uh."

"We have to go to a Justice—"

"Oh, he skipped that part, did he?" The woman shook her head, making *tsk* sounds.

"But he's older he should know better." Ula said, wide-eyed.

"Oh, he did, honey. I'm sure he did."

"They will tell you *anything* you want to hear to get in your pants. *Tsk,tsk,tsk.*"

"No. He wouldn't. He's a gentleman."

The two women burst out laughing. Using their hands, they pushed up from the curb, brushing off the seat of their jeans, still chuckling. A bus neared the stop. "Men are nice to have, baby. But only you can take care of you." Air brakes squealed as the bus stopped. The doors slapped open in front of the women. "Where you goin' to?"

"I...don't know."

"Get yourself a job." The bandana woman hefted her tool case. "You get smart real quick when you learn to stand on your own two feet." The women boarded. "Stay outta the street now," one called as she disappeared up the steps.

The driver gave Ula a questioning look. She stared back, blank-faced. The doors shooshed shut and the bus took off, leaving her in a cloud of fumes.

She didn't know how long she'd sat on the curb. It was dark when she noticed feet walking by. She felt numb and stupid and alone. Not the lying-on-dog-food alone, but for the first time in her life, she felt ain't-nobody-coming-to-rescue-me alone. She was on her own. She should go home—but which one?

Ula walked through the back door of the convent. Fresh, cool air clung to her. Droplets of mist netted her hair in the light of the kitchen.

"Where have you been?" Sister Heavé stood up, leaving Mother Radagunda sitting at the table where Ula usually ate.

Ula waited, slack-shouldered, staring at the stone-tiled floor.

The Sister clenched her fists at her side. "I said I'd be back in two shakes and I'd barely—"

Mother Radagunda laid her hand on the hefty nun's arm, giving her a silencing look. She waited until Sister Heavé's frenetic energy had sparked out of the air, then quietly said, "Sit, child."

Ula hesitated, and then took a seat across from the Mother, her eyes on the table.

"You appear chilled. I think hot broth would be the thing, don't you, Sister?"

Ula shook her head. "I don't want any, thank you."

"But you will sip it anyway to ward off the chilblains," the Mother said.

Ula barely nodded. They sat in silence until the thickset nun slid a mug of chicken broth onto the table.

"I'm sorry. I didn't get the ham. I...I'm so stupid."

Sister Heavé bent down, trying to see into Ula's eyes. "It's all right. The scoundrels only had six scrawny shanks. They were gone in minutes. Did you run because you lost the ration stamps?"

Ula's eyebrows arched upward. She patted her sweater then dug into her pocket, letting out a big breath as she pulled out the booklets.

"Then why didn't you wait?"

Ula slowly shook her head. "Why...did there have to be a war? It changed everything. If there was no war, my brother wouldn't be missing in Turkey. I wouldn't have left home. I wouldn't even be in this kitchen. My father's predictions were right. The war has torn my family apart. I've been so gullible. A half-wit."

"What's happened?" Sister Heavé took Ula's hand. "Where did you go?"

"I panicked. Ran and ran. Got lost."

"What scared you?" Mother Radagunda leaned forward as Ula looked away. "Are you all right? Should I call the police?"

Ula met her eyes. "No. Nothing like that. It's my fault. People were kind and told me how to get here. It was a long walk home. I've had plenty of time to think. I've been a child—about everything. I'm sorry I've made it hard for you."

The nuns exchanged a glance. Mother Radagunda patted Ula's hand. "You have a good heart, dear. In dark times like these, we need the strength of all good hearts. Things often look different in the light of day. We'll talk more tomorrow. For now, rest. I'm glad you're safely back with us."

After she left, Ula stared at her broth, holding the cup for warmth. Sister Heavé cleaned and described the excitement her absence had caused.

"Sister?" Ula interrupted. "Is Kol a good man?"

"Your husband?" The nun looked up from drying a bowl, her brow furrowed. "Yes, why would you ever ask that?"

"Then why did he take me away from my home and bring me here?"

"Oh." The Sister let out a long sigh. "I'm no expert on men, but I think as you get older, you'll discover—men don't always think with their heads."

The rain started in the middle of the night. A light shower. The gurgle of the drain pipe echoed against the basement walls.

Her suitcase made a soft *click* as she closed it.

The long walk home this evening had given Ula two things: a heel blister, and clarity. She figured out why she'd run. She was fleeing the truth. She'd been living a lie, deceiving the Sisters. She'd become a heartbreaking disappointment as a daughter. She was a shore-leave pastime, a slut, washing plates and sweeping floors. Taking responsibility for nothing. Not even her own stupidity.

She sneaked upstairs, placing the Beech Nut chewing gum in front of Virgin Mary. She hoped Marina would find it. She wouldn't have made it these last two months without the Novice's help. The chocolate bar would've been a better gift, but the poor girl had a thimble-sized capacity for guilt. It would've pegged her shame until she'd confessed to all their late night meetings and even blurted out sins she hadn't committed yet. A pack of gum was all the selfishness the Novice could bear.

The Captain? He wasn't her husband. She owed him nothing. He may return, but she wouldn't be waiting. Not for the man who had ruined her. She dropped his mother's wedding ring into an envelope with his name on the front, sealed it, and left it on her bedside table. Let him explain his deeds to the nuns.

She'd eaten one chocolate bar to celebrate her birthday. She left the last one for Sister Heavé. The plump nun had no problem with guilt.

In Mother Radagunda's place at the dining table, she left a note:

Thank you, and all the Sisters, for everything. I'm leaving to help stop this damn war.

Ula.

She stepped out into the soft rain, tipping her face upward, letting it wash away tears.

Leaving felt different this time.

Instead of running away—she was running toward something.

No Room In Any Manger

A t the Seattle train depot, Ula asked a few questions and was told that California was the land of opportunity, the place to go if she wanted a good-paying job and independence.

Thanks to watching Kol, she knew how to buy tickets for the San Diegan coastal line. Thanks to the nuns, she was skilled at getting information without revealing too much. Now, she followed the crowd off the train.

She walked out of the depot into warm sunshine. Everyone who wasn't in uniform headed for the Employment Office. At the large, plain building, ladies sat behind rows of wooden desks. Posters lined the walls. Ula filled out the application honestly— except for her age. A woman on the train had told her she had to be eighteen to work in a defense plant.

Have you ever used an electric drill: No

Fixed an engine: No

Painted a house or a room: No

Do you have mechanical experience? No.

A young blonde, her hair in a Victory roll from the nape of her neck to the top of her head, seemed overjoyed that Ula had come in today. "We need women. What do you want to do?"

"Why not that?" Ula pointed to a poster of an attractive gal working on the nozzle plugs of a yellow plane, then laughed at her joke. "I have no skills besides cleaning."

"That's wonderful. 'Keep 'em Flyin'. You're desperately needed. But are you willing to get your hands dirty?"

Ula held up her hands. The skin was rough and red from scrubbing with lye soap, the fingernails jagged and short.

The clerk stamped the application. "You're hired. Go see Mrs. Mapes." She pointed a polished nail at the desk behind her.

Mrs. Mapes was older. She, too, wore a Victory roll, but had a flower pinned at the top of the coil. Behind her, a poster of three women looked out on the room: a secretary, a welder and a riveter—*Soldiers Without Guns*. Mrs. Mapes worked as though the Nazis were at the gates. "Which shift do you want?"

Ula looked around, hoping for a menu or a schedule. Mrs. Mapes checked a box, whispering. "Swing Shift pays eight cents more an hour." Ula nodded.

"Wonderful. They need women on that shift. Now which plant?"

This time, it was Ula who leaned forward.

"The Main Plant starts 4:30 in the afternoon and you're off at 1 a.m.," she said quietly.

Ula nodded and was rewarded with a *Good choice!* then sent to the next station.

A few long, black strands remained on Mr. Tinner's head, testimony that he once had hair. At his station, he pushed paper after paper across the desk, mumbling, "Sign this."

"What are all these?" Ula scribbled her name.

"Money you won't be getting," he muttered. "Taxes, insurance. Union dues. Read and sign this..." He set a stern-looking document in front of her. The Espionage Act...No. 8381 was full of intimidating words: Classified, Secret, Confidential, and Restricted. It threatened fines or imprisonment for talking about such projects.

"You mean I can't tell anyone what I do?"

"Just the Confidential and Secret projects, but why would you want to talk about work at all?" He handed her a sheet of paper. "Here's what you'll need. Where to report. Start tomorrow." With a rap on the desk, he turned and waved the next new hire to his station.

A small ember of importance glowed in Ula's chest. She'd done it. She had a job. A real job at 60 cents an hour, 52 hours a week. And she might even be working on *secret* projects.

After a few inquiries, she headed to the USO Travelers Aid, where she was asked, "Did you bring a tent?" Ula shook her head. "Population has doubled in San Diego. Churches, private residences, government housing is full. Don't you have a relative or friend?" Ula shook her head again. "Check with us tomorrow. Things change every day."

Outside, Ula stood in the fading light of sunset and counted her coins. The train ticket had taken most of her savings. She'd carefully pinned the remaining dollars to her bra. Breakfast had been bread she'd taken from the nuns. There was no lunch. She still needed to buy work clothes. Staying in a hotel was out of the question.

A walking search of the nearby neighborhoods didn't reveal any "For Rent" signs. She knocked on a few doors, asking for a sleeping space, a hallway, the floor, a back porch. She received only "no's." As night fell, Ula repositioned the piece of cloth she'd put on her seeping heel blister and watched a family spread blankets in the entryway of a darkened storefront.

It had come to this. She'd left a safe bed and the irritation of being treated like a kid to gain the adult responsibility of sleeping on the street. Well, it was her choice, and she was sticking with it. She could survive for one night.

She chose a storefront next to the family—a drugstore. Its deep, recessed entry would keep her from easily being seen. Unfortunately, light leaked around the sides and bottom of its blackout curtains. It was still open. When the store closed, she'd claim a spot.

"Hey, baby! How about a sample for the men who serve your country?" Three Marines surrounded her, their faces eager.

"I'm waiting for someone."

"Well, we're here!" declared a beefy lance corporal, his arms spread wide as the others laughed.

"Go away." Ula picked up her suitcase and pushed through them toward the drugstore.

"Well, you shouldn't stand on the corner advertising if you don't want customers," a private yelled after her. "We'll pay," shouted a second soldier.

The bell *tink-tink*ed as she hurried through the door. She turned and peeked out the black curtain. The private waved his fingertips. The other two guffawed.

"Can I help you?"

Ula jumped at the sound of the female voice. "Sorry. I only stepped inside because those men were bothering me."

"New in town?" The girl asked as she opened the door and looked out. "Hey, boys! I just heard there's half-price pints at O'Reillys on Thirty-second."

"Come with us!" a Marine shouted back.

"Gotta work. Bye, fellas. Stop bothering our customers." She closed the door and headed toward the register. "They're harmless. Just treat 'em like you would a brother."

"My brother is missing in action. I'd hug and drink beer with all of them if they were my brother."

"I'm very sorry. How can I help you?"

Ula judged the girl to be slightly older and more experienced than her because she handled servicemen like they were big puppies. "I need a room for tonight—well for many nights. I just got a job."

"Sorry. No rooms. Which plant?"

"I'm building airplanes."

"There are three companies here. Which shift?"

"Four-thirty to one in the morning." Ula dug in her pocket to see if the company name was on her documents.

"That's Consolidated. Do you have your uniform? We carry them. You look like a size 7." The girl was already walking toward the back of the store. "You'll need two. One to wear, one to wash."

Ula scanned her papers. "You're right. It's Consolidated Vultee. How did you know?"

"Do you have a scarf?" She waved a hand around her head. "To protect your curls."

"It says hat." Ula pointed at the requirements.

"Creepers. Nobody wears a hat. They're ugly. You'll need a tool chest, but you'll have to go to the hardware store for that."

Ula bought one blue coverall and nothing else. She'd never even worn a pair of slacks before. As she tucked them in her suitcase, she tried to hide the crack in the side. At the door she paused, checking to be sure the street was clear of Marines. "What time do you close?"

"We don't. With two Navy bases, a Marine base, shipyards and airplane plants running around the clock, this town doesn't sleep. Why don't you try the movie house for shelter? Half the people in there are asleep, but the ushers will run you out at the end of the picture."

Ula stepped into the cloudless night, muttering a prayer for a room. Even the flophouse Kol had stuck her in looked pretty good right now. He'd been right. They'd been lucky to find it. It must've cost a fortune to keep her in a room that would sleep four.

The all-night Bijou ignored the blackout rules. A few dim bulbs flickered in each letter of its sign. Ula bought a ticket to *Double Indemnity*. She stood at the back of the theater, trying to determine how many of the twenty or more patrons were snoozing. If this movie house was like the one back in Ponca City, it might solve her problem. The trick was to look like she knew what she was doing.

Holding her suitcase flat in front of her like it was a box, she walked to the front and up the stage steps. To the right of the screen she pushed back the velvet curtain, hoping she wouldn't be staring at bricks.

A black cavernous space loomed in front of her. She slipped past the curtain and leaned against the wall, letting out the breath she'd been holding. Back home, during the weird parts of *Fantasia,* she and Patty had snuck into the backstage area which was used for plays. Unfortunately, Mary Miller, champion tattler of 7th grade, had reported them. They were rousted by an usher and greeted by the laughter of the Saturday morning licorice lickers.

Later, she and Patty had reviewed their mistakes. The first was: peeking out the curtain at the saps watching prancing pink elephants. The second was: making too much noise. They'd danced and shimmied behind the screen, delighted they were in front of an audience that couldn't see them.

Ula smiled for an instant, amazed how her stupidest experience had become survival training. She worked her way along the wall. The Bijou's backstage was piled with neglected furnishings, velvet ropes, dusty boxes, and wide brooms. By the diffused light of the screen, she made a nest in the corner, propped up in old theater seats and covered with posters. She fell into a fitful sleep, awakened every two hours by the suspenseful music that accompanied Fred McMurray's plans to kill Barbara Stanwyck's husband for insurance money.

The next morning, as she slipped out the alley door, the manager yelled at her. She ran.

Her continued search for housing rewarded her with another blister. Ula stopped at a diner in the afternoon, ordering toast and tea. The man at the counter left his corn muffin; she stuffed it in her pocket when the waitress wasn't looking. In the bathroom, she changed into her uniform before paying.

It seemed everyone in the city knew how to get to Consolidated Aircraft. Ula's bus arrived at Gate Two along with a line of buses that stretched for a half mile. Around her, thousands of people poured into the parking lot. She joined the herd crossing the wide foot bridges over the highway. Her heart knocked against her chest; she had no clue what to do; yet there was comfort in being part of a herd. Hopefully, the person leading the pack knew where to go.

"You! Stop!" A rough hand jerked her backward as she walked through a gate. "Where's your badge?" Ula looked into the eyes of an armed soldier. Another one stood nearby, his rifle ready.

"My first day," Ula stuttered, digging through her pockets for papers and pulling out the corn muffin. "It's in my suitcase." She dropped her luggage on the asphalt, fumbling at the catches.

The crowd parted and flowed around her, a few turning to watch the soldier pull her to her feet and order her inside a tall concrete wall with barbwire coiled across the top. Peeking out the barred window, she willed herself not to cry.

People opened their lunch boxes for inspection. Many of the women lugged tool boxes like the ones she'd seen the black ladies carrying in Seattle. Soldiers pulled drawer after drawer open, peering inside before they sent employees through the gate.

"Miss Haupt?" Ula flinched. She'd gone back to her maiden name. After all—she wasn't married. "Miss Haupt!" The brown-haired woman in slacks and silky blue blouse had urgency in her voice. "You didn't pick up your temporary badge yesterday. Has this been checked?" The woman hailed a soldier, who grabbed Ula's suitcase and slapped it on the inspection table, cutting in front of the next waiting employee. Ula wanted to crawl under the cement. She would've run if it hadn't meant losing everything she owned in the world. Her Bible dress and underwear lay on top. The soldier lifted the few pieces inside, shut the case, and handed it to Ula.

A red-haired gal waiting in line said, "Hillbillies," and her friends laughed.

"Follow me." The woman handed Ula a green button stamped with numbers and briskly walked away. "Mr. Stewart is waiting. Always wear your badge at work. It has your department and time clock number. No. No. Always over your heart." She tapped her chest, watching Ula double-time her steps to keep up while trying to pin on the button with a suitcase in her hand. The woman made a sharp right turn into a gray-green building, where fifty women sat clacking at typewriters.

Ula was last to join a group of people standing in the center of the room. "Okay. Let's snap to it." Mr. Stewart shot her a quick glance and launched his speech about time and the war effort, interspersed with, "Every second counts," "Matter of life and death," "Look lively," "Put your skates on." It was a nesting doll of clichés, each one growing with the urgent feeling: "Get as many planes in the air as possible, and end this war."

Without warning, he held up a pair of goggles. "You will be fitted with safety glasses. We'll grind them to your prescription if need be." Then he slammed them against the table like he was pummeling Hitler. *Whack-whack-whack.* "They'll keep you on the job. No missed time from injury. Wear them." He turned and walked away as though the whacking were a satisfying experience, and he'd completed his duty.

A tall, elegant woman in a slim brown skirt took his place, introducing herself as Mrs. Oakmont. She announced she would be speaking only to the women and shooed the men off to follow Mr. Whack-It. "Welcome. Now this is between us girls." She winked. "There are days of the month you may not feel like coming in."

Ula looked around wide-eyed. Mother Mary! They weren't going to talk about this, standing in the middle of the room, were they?"

"We encourage you to come to work. Every day counts. There are special exercises to relieve cramps." Mrs. Oakmont did a few knee lifts, marching in a small circle. "You're even allowed to work while you're pregnant—if your doctor will approve it. If you have a problem, look for the nurses on the production line, they're the only ones allowed to wear skirts." Ula missed the last thing she'd said; she was still mentally goggling about doing exercises for the monthlies out here in front of God and everyone.

"There will be charm classes once a week during the lunch period," Mrs. Oakmont continued. "You may be doing a man's job, but no one wants you to act like a man. When this war is over, you can resume your lives without worrying that you've lost any of your daintiness or feminine abilities."

A woman next to Ula gave a mirthless laugh. "I came for the money, not charm school. If every second counts, why're we listening to this crap?" Ula didn't say anything. She was actually excited to learn how to act more grown-up. Her mind traveled back to Melody on the train. She didn't seem like a hooker—what would Kol know about it?

She sneaked a sideways glance, judging the woman next to her to be in her late twenties. A nest of frizzy curls stuck out the front of her blue bandana.

"I'm Tanna." The woman grinned, catching Ula looking at her. "My husband works at Station 10."

Before Ula could respond, the group began moving, following Mrs. Oakmont outside and across the lots. Ula gawked like a tourist, her head swiveling right and left. Large dark-green buildings on either side of the walkway had fake facades with saw-toothed roofs that made them look like a neighborhood with houses. Tall trees cast long shadows over the area. Above her, netting, fuzzy with chicken feathers, covered the walkway. "To camouflage us." Tanna stared upward too. "My hubby says when they apply new feathers, everybody gets itchy with lice."

They passed a stage with red, white, and blue bunting tacked to the front. A large poster showed an airman climbing into his cockpit: *So We'll Meet Again—Buy War Bonds.* A blackboard listed those employees with good attendance who had won bonds in the latest company drawing.

At another fake-fronted building, several men waited to take employees to various departments. Ula and Tanna were assigned to Mr. Dillard, a tall, stoop-shouldered man with worry lines etching his face. The ladies followed him into Building 4. It took a moment for their eyes to adjust from the afternoon sunlight to the fluorescents inside.

Ula came to a standstill, her mouth open.

Tool Boxes and Tail Sections

T he place seemed to be an endless cavern. Above them, the ceiling faded into darkness. Planes in various stages of completion stretched in a horseshoe line, morphing into shadowy forms on the other side of the room.

People crawled over hulky frames, reminding Ula of bees on a watermelon. Platforms stood under the wings and belly of each plane. Heads poked out of open nose cones. Men and women walked along the dull gray tops of fuselages. Some stuck their bodies through windows, banging on the sides; others wedged into massive engines. Workers went in and out of every opening. Wrenches clanged, motors hummed, and drills squealed, piercing sheet metal with rivets. The sounds blended and dampened into mechanical murmurs in the vacuous size of the room.

Tanna reached out and grabbed Ula, jerking her forward to keep up. "Bombers?" The whites of Ula's eyes got bigger as she stumbled forward. "I can't..."

"B-25s." Mr. Dillard grinned, giving Ula a sideways glance. "Majestic, aren't they? You can. We'll teach you."

"My Wally works over there," Tanna pointed to the other side of the building. She looked up, searching for numbers as they walked down the wide center aisle.

Mr. Dillard stopped and both women ran into him. "Pay attention," he ordered as a ceiling crane slowly crossed in front of them, dangling a nose cone from its steel cable. A girl on a bicycle pulled to a stop next to Ula. A man and a woman grabbed the cone, hauling it into position. The girl pedaled off as soon as it was out of her way. Mr. Dillard motioned the two ladies to the side of the aisle, and waited as a truck loaded with oxygen bottles passed.

As they walked down the line, the metal fuselages changed at each station, becoming more plane-like and laden with destruction. They reminded her of when the circus came to town. Like the line of elephants, the planes followed each other nose to tail. She wondered if the one at the end of the line, the "finished" ones, had showy teeth painted on them and glittered with guns.

Ula was sure she couldn't find her way back out of the building, much less where she was supposed to work each day. She looked for landmarks—like the time clock. They continued walking another third of a mile. She lost count of how many time clocks she passed. First aid huts and offices huddled at intervals. The *ding-ding* of another bike told them to stop pointing, keep their arms and legs close, they were being passed. At each station, women and men climbed ladders into planes with loops of electric cords and hoses over their shoulders.

An ache began to tap the front of Ula's skull. It was too much to take in. She focused on her feet, trying not to see anything new. When they stopped, Ula ran into Tanna. "Sorry."

"Over there is the tool crib. This is your time clock. Always use this one. Your department number and clock number are on your badge." Mr. Dillard touched his red badge over his heart. "Punch in." Ula stepped aside, watching Tanna stick her card in a slot. The machine made a *clunka-clunk* sound. Ula copied her, relieved when she heard the *clunka-clunk*. She was sure it would jam or explode as soon as she touched it. "I hope I can find my card again." she said with a nervous laugh, sticking it into the "In" rack.

"The timekeeper alphabetizes them," Tanna whispered as they waited for Mr. Dillard to read their records. "It's her job to come looking for you about three times a day to make sure you're really here. My Wally says they get to the point they can identify you by your shoelaces."

"Miss Haupt, Mrs. Higgenloop," the timekeeper called the girls to her window. She scanned them up and down. "See the girders?" She pointed upward. "The numbers tell you where you are on the line. It's easy to get lost. Look at the numbers on your badge if you forget." You won't find your time cards anywhere except your own clock. Important to remember if you want to get paid." She gave them both one more head to toe scan. Ula wondered how the woman was cataloguing her: Short, frog-skin shoes, looking as lost as a cow at an opera.

"Put your lunch boxes over there." Mr. Dillard pointed to a collection of arched-topped lunch pails in a bin. Tanna dropped hers off. Ula didn't move.

"That your lunch box or a tool kit?" Mr. Dillard pointed at Ula's suitcase which seemed as large and logical to be carrying as an oven.

"Uh...no. I didn't... have a chance...." She looked away. "It's my suitcase."

"Well, put it over there unless it has tools in it you need." Ula dropped it next to lunch pails, sure that it had turned bright orange and was flashing to get attention.

"You girls will need to buy tool boxes and tools," Mr. Dillard said. "You can borrow some for today. Ohio follow me." The women stared at him as he walked several yards then turned around. "Your papers say you're from Ohio. Aren't you?" He looked at Tanna.

She shook her head. "Not anymore. That's where I was born."

"C'mon Ohio." He walked off, waving for her to join him.

Ula followed. She wasn't sure if "Ohio" meant her too, but she didn't want to be left alone.

They climbed a ladder into the tail of a plane. "You wait here." He pointed at Ula as he and Tanna entered.

Ula peeked after them. The tail was a long metal tube with people bent in various positions banging, drilling, or twisting tools. She couldn't hear what Mr. Dillard was saying, but by watching, it seemed the gist of Tanna's job was feeding wires through holes so a young man could solder them to a switch. Ula felt jealous. That looked easy. She could do that job.

Everyone appeared to be "making every second count." A young man lay on his stomach busily arranging hoses between floor girders. Another man twisted a ratchet wrench. A woman concentrated on easing tubing around a window opening.

When Ula saw Mr. Dillard returning, she quickly pulled her head out of the plane's door and concentrated on the numbers above her: Station 18.

"C'mon Li'l Okie." He passed her, clumping down the ladder like they were steps. Ula had to turn around and descend backwards, like she always had on a ladder.

"You cannot work on a ship without covering your hair." He glanced at Ula's unruly shoulder-length bob which looked like it hadn't seen a comb in a couple of days.

Some of the women at the plant had their hair flowing free. One even had a big bow in it. Ula didn't argue. She'd meant to tie it back Candidate-style this morning, but had forgotten.

"You'll be in here—assembling aviator seats for now. You need twelve ¼ by 2-inch hex bolts, lock washers, and hex nuts. The bins haven't been replenished yet, so you'll have to run over to parts. Got that?"

"Um...no."

"You can't stick any bolt in any hole. Learn the names of parts. You have to use the right part if you want the plane to hold together."

Ula swallowed and nodded, her eyes shiny, hoping her brother's plane hadn't been built by idiots like her.

"Here." Mr. Dillard's voice softened. He wrote the list on a paper bag, then dropped the parts inside. "Memorize these."

She took off, only to return a moment later. "I'm sorry, I forgot. Where's the parts place, please?"

He pointed without looking up from the chart at his bench area.

Ula navigated between cables and large humming machines. "Cover below!" someone yelled. A wrench dropped, grazing her shoulder.

"You okay?" A thin man in his late twenties peered over the edge of a wing, concern on his face. Ula looked up and nodded, rubbing the top of her shoulder.

"You sure? Go to the infirmary have them check it."

That was the last thing she needed. On the job an hour and already in the infirmary. "I shouldn't have been taking a shortcut under the planes. I'm all right."

"Okay, but that had to hurt like a sonofagun. Mind handing me my wrench before you go? You know how people take tools if you let 'em lay too long."

Ula stood on her tiptoes stretching it up to him. Her arm hurt. It was going to leave quite a bruise.

"Thanks. I'm Skinny Delbert." He gave her a wink and disappeared back over the edge of the wing.

Ula had dropped the paper bag. She got on her hands and knees, searching the dusty floor, but only found half of the scattered pieces.

The crib was a small caged room. The people in line in front of her plunked their bolts and cotter pins at the window saying, "I need four of these things." Obviously, knowing parts was only important to foremen. Ula vowed to memorize the names of what she needed anyway. Next time she might be hit with something that would make her lose the whole bag.

When she made it back, Mr. Dillard asked, "Okay. Now, have you ever used a drill?" She shook her head. He showed her how to put two holes in the metal brace for each side of the seat, then how to attach the back to the bottom with a ratchet wrench. "Now you do the next one; I'll watch."

Ula gripped the drill, its handle wrapped with tape. When she placed the bit on the brace and pulled the trigger, the point shot off to the right, etching a shallow line in the metal.

She repositioned the drill. "Push hard. Hold it in place," Mr. Dillard ordered. Ula did. A tiny curlicue of metal spiraled up from the point. "Give it some juice." Mr. Dillard worked his trigger finger back and forth. Ula did. The bit skewed off to the right again, leaving another scar on the metal.

On the third try she finally punched through the plate. Her hand was sweating and her wrist shaking. "Now three more of those and put in the nuts and bolts. Call me when you're done." She winced when he gave her sore shoulder a couple of pats as he walked away.

Forty-five minutes later she had him check her work.

"Well, that's a start." He tested a bolt with a wrench. "You got 'em pretty tight. Put a little more muscle in it and give each one another half-twist. Drill your holes in straight lines so it doesn't look like you were drunk when you put it together. It gives the fly boys more confidence."

While he was talking, a loud bell rang throughout the plant. Ula strained to hear what he was saying. It cut off, but no one was running for the exit like the place was on fire.

"Lunch," he announced as he walked away.

Ula peeked from her alcove. The lunch bin had been rolled to Station18. People were pulling their pails from it. Ula was mortified to see her suitcase in the bin. She slowly stepped backward, away from the door. The cornbread muffin in her coveralls had been pulverized, leaving a greasy stain on the pocket front. She turned the material inside out, shaking crumbs into a paper bag. Putting the aviator seat into a corner, she sat and ate.

Her head still throbbed. Her shoulder ached. Her arms felt weak, her fingers numb from the vibrating drill. Staring at nothing, she said a little prayer, and added one for whoever would be sitting in this chair during the war. Then she fell asleep.

First Day At Work

The sound of a drill awakened Ula. She looked up at the bear-sized man standing over her. He had a thick patch of brown hair and hands so massive it made the drill in his fist look like a child's toy.

"Oh! Oh! I'm sorry." Ula tried to push out of her seat, but he stood too close.

"Don't get up on my account, princess." He watched her struggle to get around him. "But if a damn Red Button catches you, he'll toss you outta here on your can." He stuck out a big paw. Ula took it, and he pulled her to her feet, catching her against his chest. "I'm Gator. What's your name?"

Ula pushed off of him, freeing herself, stumbling over the aviator seat as she stepped away. She glanced outside the alcove; people were working all over the ship. "I...I didn't hear the bell. I guess I drifted off. I slept in a chair last night."

"Ya need a bed, huh? I might be able to help ya out." He grinned.

"No...thank you. I—"

"Mr. Gaither. Why am I not surprised to find you here?" Mr. Dillard stood in the doorway. "Where are you *supposed* to be?"

"Just came to get a drill, boss." He waggled the tool in the air.

"She needs that." The foreman crossed the room, holding out his hand. He stood eye-to-eye with Gator, but looked like a stick beside a giant tree. The big man slapped the drill into the Red Button's upheld palm and walked away.

Mr. Dillard handed the tool to Ula. "Don't give up anything you don't want to. Anything. You got that?" He gave her a pointed look, but she wasn't listening. She stared at Gator who had stopped at the door, one finger to his lips in a silent *Shhh!* Then he pointed at her, his fingers like a cocked gun, and winked.

The foreman turned in time to see him hurry out the door. Ula moved to the work bench and began drilling holes again.

She slugged her way through the rest of her shift, slapping her cheeks to keep awake. When the quitting bell rang at one in the morning, she proudly looked at the five seats she'd made and beamed when Mr. Dillard said, "Each one's an improvement. You can install them tomorrow. That'll be fun." He said it like it would be anything but a good time. "Now hide 'em. Throw a tarp over those before you straighten your area and punch out."

Ula silently groaned. Why couldn't she leave this for the person on the next shift? If she'd known she had to straighten up, she would've spent the last half hour doing it instead of drilling holes.

After organizing the work area, she waved a go-to-hell hand at the seats. Her arms could barely lift the drill again, much less pop open a heavy canvas tarpaulin.

Punching out and lugging her suitcase with both hands, she joined the throng headed toward the gates. She hoped there was a different manager and a different film at the Bijou tonight.

The windows of the Traveler's Aid were dark. She had stopped after work, hoping that a city short on beds and rooms would keep the Housing office open all hours. Ula shook her head as she checked her watch. Seven hours until the lights came on.

The parking lot was vacant except for a truck. Two men laughed and talked as they pushed cartons to the tailgate then hopped to the pavement. One grabbed a box and lugged it into the building, leaving the door propped open. After looking at a clipboard, the second man carried a box inside. Ula followed as stealthily as she could for a woman with a suitcase.

They turned down a hallway. She went the opposite direction and squeezed beneath the first desk she came to. After several minutes, the men walked by. The door shut and locked. The sound of the truck's engine faded as it turned a corner. Ula listened to the silence. It was comforting—like being in her room back at the convent. She sat until her bottom became numb, her knees cramped, and she was sure no one else was in the building. Crawling from under the desk on her hands and knees, she groaned. Her legs were stiff, her arms half-dead, and her bruised shoulder ached.

A small tin of crackers sat on top of one the desks. She tried to eat only a few, but couldn't stop. The empty tin found a new home on top of a bookshelf of official-looking manuals. Snooping through other desks, she collected a handful of mints, a bag of peanuts, and a date bar.

Scouting the building, she deemed the custodian's closet was the most promising hideout because it had a lock. She secured the door and lay on the floor, eating peanuts, reminding herself this is what adults do—live with their choices. No matter where she slept, she was sure it was better than what Joe would have in a POW camp—if he was still alive.

Sometime later, the rattle of the door awakened her. It took a moment to get her bearings. She'd slept until noon. She doubted if she'd even moved. Peanuts were still in her hand. Stuffing the food in her coverall pockets, she stood, suitcase in hand, waiting for the lock to click, and the door to swing open.

They took too long. She opened the door and peeked out. The hallway was clear. Heading for the back door, she passed a matronly woman with keys and a young lady tagging behind, apologizing profusely for bothering her. Ula was ready to ask

"Where's the toilet?" if the women stopped her, but they marched by, their vision fogged by inconvenience and intimidation. Ula felt bad. It was going to be even worse for the young office girl when they discovered the door wasn't locked. She hesitated.

In front of her, the office was full of bags, suitcases, and travelers. A clerk was shaking her head at each person who approached her desk. Ula looked over her shoulder. "Sorry, girl," she mumbled. "At least they won't make you scrub pots for being wrong." She hurried her good intentions out the door.

Getting through the gates at Consolidated on her second evening of work was less terrifying than before. She had her badge. She made sure her underwear was on bottom when the guards inspected her luggage. Cripes! How she hated the suitcase. The crack had grown longer, the corners abraded, and no one else was toting around their clothes.

Surprisingly, she found her station, looking at the numbers on the girders. Workers checked the chart over Mr. Dillard's work table; then they took off, seemingly aware of what to do. Soon the plane was noisy with tools and people. Ula retreated to her alcove so she wouldn't look like an idiot with her hands in her pockets.

Her seats were gone. "Where's your head covering?" Mr. Dillard called from the doorway, his voice a little too loud for a casual question.

Ula pawed her hair. "I forgot."

"And it looks like the Day Shift found your seats. Installed them on their ships."

Confusion lined Ula's face. "The Navy uses these seats too?"

"We don't call them planes. They're ships that sail airways instead of water. Certain ships are assigned to each shift. The Night Shift is good. But when the Day Shift, which is a bunch of ham-fisted loafers, found your seats, they put them in their ships, so they wouldn't have to make any."

"But it all goes to the same war, doesn't it? It gets the planes—ships—in the air faster, no matter who gets credit for it. Right?"

Mr. Dillard let out a long sigh. "Let's see if you feel the same way after tonight. Make more seats. We're behind. And if you arrive tomorrow without a head wrap, I'll send you home."

Ula didn't see why only women had to cover their heads. Oh sure, she'd seen the posters of a gal's long locks caught in gears, but lots of women had short Victory bobs. Some of the men working here had hair longer than hers.

Instead of arguing, Ula nodded mutely, and set up her work station. The Day Shift had left no parts and the drill was missing. By the time she rounded up everything she needed, the whistle for the first break blew at 6:30 p.m. She worked through it, feeling the pressure of being even further behind than when she started.

She drilled through part of her half-hour lunch too. Mostly because it didn't take long to eat her stolen date bar and peanuts. Before quitting time, Mr. Dillard stuck his head in the doorway. "How many you got?"

"Seven. I don't know where to hide them. Someone took my tarp."

Mr. Dillard inspected the seats then stuck his head out the alcove, calling to a thin man standing with his tool chest in hand. "Hey. I got something for you to do." The guy checked his watch before ambling forward. "Grab these seats. Help me stow 'em on the ship." Mr. Dillard ordered.

The men made several trips. Ula grabbed one too, although she could barely lift it, her arms were so tired. When she got to the tail section, she bucked the seat up the ladder, one rung at a time.

"Here, lemme help." The thin dark-haired fellow took her seat, his long legs easily mounting the ladder two rungs at a time. The quitting whistle blew. Everyone headed for the doors. Ula waited. It seemed wrong to take off while others helped with her job. In a few minutes both men returned. "You don't remember me, do you?" the skinny fellow drawled.

Ula looked him over. He was strong, able to carry two seats at a time, but he didn't appear to own a single muscle. He looked like a tall, gangly version of Humphrey Bogart.

"I bombed you with a wrench yesterday. You have that checked?"

She shook her head. Too many other body parts hurt to notice a bruise.

"Well, I'm sure sorry. My name's Delbert. Most folks call me Skinny Delbert, cause there's a Fat Delbert working here." He grinned, picking up his tool chest and walking to the time clock. "You must be Suitcase."

Ula felt her cheeks burn. "My name is Ula. Why do people make fun when they don't know the whole story?" She rubbed her face and groaned, "I'm sorry. I'm exhausted and having problems finding housing."

"Where you staying?"

"I really don't know from night to night."

"That's tough." *Clunka-clunk.* He slipped his time card into the "Out" rack. Ula noticed Gator, leaning against the wall, watching her as he gabbed with another fellow. He pistol-pointed at her and grinned. Ula pretended not to notice. She clocked out and walked close to Delbert, passing the incoming Night Shift.

"You got a fella?" He finally spoke, looking up as though checking the stars, but there was only chicken wire and feathers overhead.

Ula considered the question. Was it over if "the fella" didn't know it yet? And was Delbert asking because he was interested in the job? She wasn't ready to take on that whole ball of worms again.

"Well, if you ever decide, lemme know." He shrugged. "Where's your suitcase?"

"Oh...crap!" Ula turned and ran back to Building 4.

When she finally left the gates, her skinny Humphrey Bogart wasn't in sight. The light-headed feeling she'd fought all day made her sit on the curb. She'd have to use a few precious coins to eat tonight, or she wouldn't make it to payday—three nights away.

She nibbled a piece of toast piled with as much chutney as she could load on top. She'd learned to eat it at the convent. Not even the clever Sister Heavé could get enough sugar to make jam, so she used the bits and ends of vegetables and fruits to make the spicy condiment. Every restaurant was using the same food rationing trick.

Looking out the diner's plate glass windows, she tried to stretch her time in the warmth by avoiding eye contact with the waitress and making herself small and invisible. Outside, fog ghosted the air, dulling the slits of light escaping from the drugstore. Drat! She had to buy a bandana.

Her stomach clutched. There went her bed at the Bijou tonight. Maybe she could find a way to sneak inside. She wasn't ready to leave, but the woman in the next booth had left the hard outer ring of a cinnamon roll. Ula nabbed it, paid her ticket, and crossed the street.

The bell *tink-tink*ed as Ula entered the drugstore. She smiled, thinking that places and sounds were becoming familiar. Even the same girl was working the register. "It's nice to see you. I'm surprised you work late."

The girl gave her a confused look. "My dad owns the store. Daryl, the night clerk, took a defense job so, of course, I have to fill in all hours, all days because all this—" she circled her hand in a *whoop-ti-do* loop, "will be mine someday. Whattya need?"

"A bandana."

The girl looked Ula up and down, pausing at the frog-skin shoes. "I remember you now. I sold you that uniform you're wearing. I said you'd need a scarf, didn't I?" The girl waved toward stacks of the blue and red folded squares. You sure you don't need anything else? You look like you could use a little Alka-Seltzer. Did you ever find a room?"

Ula shook her head. "I'm sleeping in doorways." It wasn't quite a lie—she might have to camp out tonight. Maybe she'd gain some sympathy from the druggist's daughter, who probably had lots of nice warm rooms at her house.

The girl held a bandana next to Ula's face. First a red one, then a blue one. "You know who you should talk to? You want the blue one. It brings out your eyes. You should talk to Mrs. Bell. She was just in here an hour ago, buying Nervine. She's only in her thirties, but nervous as a rabbit at a cat convention. She's worried about money. I know she has boarders right now. Maybe she's in a tight spot, and she'd put you up in her washroom or fruit cellar until you find something else."

"I'll try anything." Ula followed her to the register. "Do you have any bandanas on sale? The color doesn't matter."

"This one's ripped. It's half-price."

"I don't see any holes." Ula tried to smooth it flat on the counter.

The girl grabbed it and stuck it in a paper sack. "It's torn. If all this is mine someday, I don't want that torn scarf in the inheritance."

Ula blinked back tears, surprised how the smallest kindness cut a trench in her heart.

Using a stubby pencil barely an inch long, the girl wrote an address on the bag. "Go see her right now. I'm sure she's up.

She says she barely sleeps. Tap real lightly, or you'll scare her to death. Tell her I sent you, or she might call the police."

The house was six blocks away in an old, but maintained, neighborhood. Ula shot off a prayer, surprised that she prayed more now than she had around the nuns. A light was on somewhere in the back of the house. Wicker chairs without cushions sat on the porch. A gold star hung in the window. Ula understood why Mrs. Bell was anxious and needed money. She'd lost someone to the war—probably a husband.

She climbed two steps and took a slow breath. Staying at a convent had taught her it was possible for the knock to be a code, preparing folks on the other side of the door for what was coming.

Using one knuckle, she knocked once, the sound spreading and echoing through the house. Ula let it fade, allowing silence—pregnant with anticipation—to build. Then she made three urgent raps.

Dural Down

*U*la strained to hear footsteps. No sound came from inside. Her watch showed 2:30 in the morning. She lifted her hand to knock again and came face to face with eyes peeking through a lace curtain.

"Oh!" She stepped back. "You scared me."

The door didn't open. The head of a short woman was outlined through the lace.

"The girl at the drugstore sent me." Ula called out, feeling her heart thump against her hand on her chest. "She said you needed a boarder, and I'd be perfect."

The silhouette of the head disappeared. No lights came on. No sound came from inside.

"Look. I'm exhausted. I'm sitting on your porch until you decide it's safe to talk to me." Ula flopped into one of the wicker chairs, rubbing her arms as the chilly fog soaked into her bones.

After ten minutes, the porch light flicked on. Ula was in the process of slipping her black dress adorned with Bible verses over her coveralls. She turned toward the door, but couldn't see anything; the bodice of the dress covered her head like a shroud. "Is someone there?"

Mrs. Bell only stared.

Ula finished yanking the dress down to her waist. "I was cold," she said flatly, too tired to be embarrassed or proud.

Mrs. Bell's voice was barely louder than the fog. "Come in." She clutched her chenille robe with both hands as though she had fistfuls of her heart in her grip.

Ula entered, and when waved to the living room, she took a seat on a foot stool. "My pants are dirty. I don't want to sit on your good furniture."

"I don't know how good it is anymore," Mrs. Bell whispered. "It's become worn, I'm afraid." She remained standing.

Ula covered her mouth and a large yawn. "Sorry. I've been looking for a room for three days. I have a job at Consolidated Vultee."

"I called Kathy at the drugstore. She said you seemed all right." Mrs. Bell let go of her chest and began rubbing her hands. "I have an extra bed. The problem...and it *is* a problem...Big Mae would have to approve of you."

"Who's Big Mae?"

Mrs. Bell held a finger in front of her mouth and lowered her voice even more. "One of the boarders. You'd be her roommate, but she considers it her room. She's a bit rough. She has run off several people."

"I've hardly slept in three days. I'll wake her up and convince her." Ula stood. "If she throws me out the window, I don't care. Which bedroom is she in?"

"Oh! Oh!" Mrs. Bell fluttered her hands, motioning for Ula to sit. "She's not like that, well... she can be. But she's not here. None of the girls are. They must've gone somewhere after work. They know how that upsets me, but they do it anyway." She stopped rubbing her hands and clutched her robe again. "I worry about them. We can wait until Big Mae gets in then ask."

Ula nodded. The room fell silent. Too tired for conversation, she stretched her legs in front of her and rubbed her back, looking at the furnishings. A small couch and matching chair surrounded a coffee table. A *Life* magazine lay open next to a reading lamp. Its full page ad for Lux Soap flakes promised it was the way to *Stay Fresh* and *Get a Man*. "Saaaay..." Ula broke the silence, "would it be all right if I rinsed out these coveralls, while I'm waiting?"

"Well...I don't—"

"Where's the laundry? Through here?" Ula knew she was being overbearing, but she didn't care anymore. There was a limit to being tired and dirty and smelling like everything she'd eaten in the last few days. Besides, she doubted if the meek Mrs. Bell would fuss too much. She walked through the kitchen toward the closed-in porch. "Even if Big Mae doesn't approve, I'd be so thankful to start tomorrow with a clean uniform. This may be my last chance to wash for a while. I'm begging you, please?" Mrs. Bell followed making small noises of indecision.

"This is wonderful. Thank you so much. May I use a bit of soap?" Ula held up the box of Borax next to the deep metal sink on legs.

"Shhh. Someone's sleeping upstairs," Mrs. Bell said, trying to turn away, but mesmerized by Ula sliding out of her coveralls while leaving her dress on and never exposing anything but arms and legs.

When Ula's uniform, panties, and red socks hung, dripping from the line strung across the porch, Mrs. Bell offered her tea. "I can't afford coffee."

"Just a cup of hot water would be wonderful." Ula was ready to get away from the woman's vigil. "I'll wait on the couch," she said as she walked out of the room.

Mrs. Bell watched the teakettle so it wouldn't whistle. She put a tea bag on the saucer just in case the girl wanted it. Such a terribly thin-looking little soul. Pale. Dark circles under her eyes. She had a definite accent. Texas? People were arriving every day from those hard-hit states with nothing but two sticks to rub together. Who would've thought one of them would knock at her door? The extra money would be nice...but...

Her husband would know what to do if he were here. Steam twined into the air as she poured water into the cup. But he wasn't here. Never again.

She carried the tray to the living room and found Ula slouched on the couch, her head thrown back, her mouth open—sound asleep.

Mrs. Bell gently set the tray down. No need to wake her. Big Mae would be home soon. She'd let her decide.

In the meantime, she'd wait.

She'd become good at waiting.

"Oh *hell* no!" A hulky woman exclaimed, ignoring the two ladies and Mrs. Bell trying to hush her. "I am *not* rooming with that." She pointed at a girl, leaning sideways like a rag doll, her black dress with Bible verses splayed around her.

Ula never stirred. Deep in her dreams, she was back home in the swing under the old maple. Her father called and she went inside with nary a complaint.

Something sharp poked Ula's cheek. She rubbed her face and sunk back into mental blackness. In a moment, it bit again. Opening one eye, she saw a boy sticking her with the straw-strand of a broom. She pushed his arm away, looking around. Someone had covered her with a blanket.

"She's awake," yelled the kid. His Brylcreem-slicked hair failed to paste down his cowlick. He went bouncing away, knickknacks rattling on the shelves.

Ula jerked fully awake and checked her watch. Noon. She hadn't missed work. Following the voices toward the kitchen, she hesitated in the doorway.

Mrs. Bell pointed, making introductions. "Good morning. Meet Peggy." A young blonde stood at the counter, her hair in pink curling rods. She looked up from spreading peanut butter on toast and waved. Ula waved back, staring at the peanut butter. "And this is Wilhelmina. She's our married woman. Her husband is somewhere in Europe right now."

"Sardinia." Mina corrected. "His last letter talked about how much he hated sardines."

"We used to have two Mae's living here, but one...uh..." Mrs. Bell glanced at the big-boned woman. "...Little Mae left. This is Big Mae."

And she was. Standing at six feet, her shoulders were as broad as her hips. Her hands seemed almost as big as the toaster she yanked a slice of browned bread from. She scowled at Ula. "No deal, Lucille. I don't need a roommate."

"Her name is Eulalia." Mrs. Bell's hands flittered like a butterfly unable to decide where to land. But she goes by Ula for short. Like Oooo-la-la." She smiled the hope of levity.

The only response she got was from the boy, moving his head back and forth, sing-songing, "*Oooo-Laa-Laa. Oooo-La-La.*"

"Lindell." His mother warned, but the boy kept repeating it softly. She wrung her hands looking between Ula and Big Mae. "I'm sorry it didn't work out."

"At least I had one night of safe sleep. I can't thank you enough. I'll get my things." She threaded through the kitchen, pretending she didn't see Mina elbow Big Mae. As soon as she walked into the laundry room, all the women whispered at once, their hushed voices sounding like paper rattling in the wind.

Ula stepped into her coveralls, amazed at the pleasure that fresh clothes brought her. If she were back at the convent, she'd wash every dish, apron, and towel without complaint just for the feeling of cleanliness.

She gave a nun's warning knock on the doorframe before entering the kitchen. The women stopped talking and gazed at the floor or their teacups. Lindell was the only one looking at her, his face eager.

"Here, take my seat. At least have a piece of toast for breakfast." Mrs. Bell got up.

Ula lowered herself into the vacated chair, the padded vinyl seat still warm. The aroma of peanuts made her stomach growl.

"You work at Consolidated Vultee?" Mina pointed to Ula's uniform, but didn't wait for an answer. "Me, too. Nuts! I forgot to rinse mine out last night."

"Got the job three days ago. I'm on Swing," Ula pitched her voice louder as the woman left the room.

" 'We're the Janes that make the planes!' I work at Rohr." Peg pumped a fist. "We're all on swing, except sourpuss here." She pointed at Big Mae. "She works at the shipyard and considers it night shift because they get out an hour later. Keeps the buses from being jam packed."

"You eat like a pig!" Lindell called out, leaning toward Ula, his hands gripping the edge of the table.

Big Mae smacked his head. "Shut up, ya little shit." He dived under the table.

"Apologize, Lindell!" demanded Mrs. Bell, bending to harangue the boy. Ula stared at her empty, oily fingers. She thought she was nibbling, but she didn't even remember eating the toast.

"Have another piece before you go." Big Mae pushed a plate of stacked slices toward her.

"Oh, Lord. Take it!" wailed Peg. "Everyone! Come see this. Big Mae just shared something." She laughed, but Ula wasn't paying attention.

Lindell was poking her with the broom-straw again. Lightly at first, then harder and harder. Ula knew the game. She'd played a lifetime of it with her brother. He'd keep poking her until she jumped.

Reaching beneath the table, she pinched Lindell's ear, dragging him out. "Stop it, kid. That hurts." When she let go, he waggled the straw at her. "You poke me again with anything," she snatched it from his fingers, "I'll pierce your ears with it before I leave." She added one of Mother Radagunda's stares. The boy backed away.

"Apologize, Lindell. You know better," Mrs. Bell ordered without much conviction.

"Sorry!" He demanded, making a face as he took off. Big Mae smacked the back of the head as he left the room.

The big woman stood and carried her dishes to the sink. Her body filled the kitchen. "Ooooo-La? What a kind of name is that?" She paused at the doorway. "Well, Ooooo-La, I think, between you and me, we might be able to knock some sense into that brat." She left, her footsteps thudding up the stairs.

Peg and Mina clapped and grinned. Mrs. Bell began unwrapping a loaf of Wonder Bread. "I'll get your sandwiches made. Pick out your apples."

Ula looked around.

"You're in." Peg shook Ula's bruised shoulder. "You're in!"

"Run while you can." Mina dumped the crusts of her toast into the trash can. "You've just jumped from the fire into the frying pan."

Mrs. Bell provided her boarders with one meal a day: A dinner of spam and mayo on white bread with a small apple. "It's the same each day," whispered Peg.

It sounded like heaven to Ula. "I'll just put my sandwich in my pocket." She frowned at the empty Swift can Mrs. Bell had stuck it in when she discovered Ula didn't have a lunch pail. "I'm already known as 'Suitcase.' I don't want to be renamed 'Lard Can.'"

"That's you?" Mina laughed then covered her mouth. "Sorry. The Reds were talking about you. I'm in the same building. Station 40. It'll be a mess if you put it in your pocket. Take the can. It's better than the suitcase. Trust me."

The bus ride to work was easier. It was still crowded, but Ula was amazed at what she'd gotten used to: elbowing through crowds, hanging onto a strap, women conductors, and bumping against strangers. Dressing like others made it easier too. Her uniform fit in—especially now that it wasn't stained by cornmeal muffins and stolen pieces of sweet roll. Her head was covered with the universal bandana. And now her lunch pail was smaller than a bread box.

Walking toward Building 4, the warning whistle blew. Ula walked faster, but Mina didn't. "We'll make it. Don't worry," she said, ambling at the same pace as hundreds of others carrying tool boxes. Ula reached the time clock, hurriedly scanning for her time card, but not finding it.

"Oh good Lord," exclaimed a redheaded woman, ripping the card out of the rack, shoving it at her.

Ula gave her a burning look. "I would've found it."

"Hillbillies!" The redhead didn't lower her voice as she clocked in. Neither did the two ginger-haired women who laughed loudly at her joke.

At Mr. Dillard's work table, people scanned the chart, looking to see where they should start. Lights went on in every other ship. Noise lulled in anticipation of the whistle. When it blew, the scree of drills, the bang of hammers, and the hum of industry began.

Someone was already installing Ula's pilot seats, so Mr. Dillard assigned her to string-tying. They climbed the ladder into the tail. A few people with wrenches kneeled on the floor. Workers straddled them. Some used ladders, others balanced on hand rails, attaching tubes to the ceiling. Everywhere someone was squeezed into a cranny, working as though the sand was almost through the hourglass.

Mr. Dillard showed Ula how to make an electrician's hitch, assuring her it was easy for women because they had small fingers and could work them into narrow places. "Tie strings around the wire bundles running along beltframes." He left, and Ula noticed the frenzied work pace slowed considerably.

She didn't hurry either, but by the time the whistle blew for Smoking—a ten minute break at 6:30 p.m.—her fingers felt as though she'd rubbed away her fingerprints. Multiple wires ran through the ship. She'd crawled on her hands and knees through the narrow passage above the life rafts. She'd stretched on tiptoe over windows and kneeled on the metal corrugated flooring—from the nose of the ship to the tail

When the lunch whistle blew at 8:30, she felt both relief and overwhelming confidence. Talla joined her and her lard can, sitting next to the outer wall, admiring her work. The ships, platforms, and ladders began inching forward at a slug's pace. A piece of her Spam sandwich fell from her mouth. She quickly picked it up and stuck it back in, hoping Tanna hadn't seen it. "Cripes. Everything's moving."

"Yeah, the line moves at lunch," Tanna said. "I didn't notice it the first night I was here. I just went back to the same ship I'd been working on, but nobody was there. They like to watch the shock on the newbies' faces." Ula's stomach turned sour. She wanted the hideous wire-tying job to be finished—not start on a new ship.

After lunch, Mr. Dillard complimented the job she'd done. "Do I have to work on that new ship?" She could hear the whine in her voice.

"No, Li'l Okie." She was relieved he didn't call her Suitcase like the rest of the workers. "You stay on this ship. Start at the command deck and tie the wires on the other side." She let out a long groan. He walked off with a shrug. "Sounds like fun to me."

She wasn't alone; most of the workers were still finishing their installations. During the last break, she lay down, right where she was in the bomb bay, the ribs in the metal floor finding every sore muscle in her back. Only three nights into her job, and she'd lost all zeal for the war effort.

The last hour of the day moved like a glacier. She'd only progressed halfway aft—toward the tail end—when a woman's sweet, high voice singing "Sentimental Journey" came from a wing. From the opposite wing, a man answered, singing the next stanza in a deep baritone. Ula stood up, her head protruding from the bomb bay through the flooring. Peeking into the long recesses on either side of the ship, she saw a man in the right wing and woman in the left. On their backs, lamps hooked to beltframes, they worked inches from their faces, soldering wires and serenading the ship. When the song ended, someone requested another. "As Time Goes By" floated through the fuselage.

Ula sank to the bottom of the bomb bay. Tension slid from her shoulders. For the first time, music affected her. It had power. It wasn't just hymns repeated over and over until the words were rote. The music calmed. It soothed. It assured her she could keep going when there wasn't anything left.

"Dural!"

Ula looked up in time to see shining flecks raining down and get a face full of metal drillings.

"Don't rub your eyes!" A woman ordered. "Cry it out."

The lightweight, durable metal of the fuselage—duralumin—speckled her face and sifted through her hair. "Listen, Suitcase. When you hear *Dural* or *Sawdust below* keep your head down. It's a warning."

"Just keep cryin', honey," a woman said. "We've all gotten a nose full of it. It took me a month not to look up when somebody above yelled. One time it was pliers that somebody dropped. Now I just cover my head when they yell. You'll get the hang of it."

Ula heard her name called, but before she could answer someone said, "Yeah, she's bawling down in the bomb bay."

The timekeeper peeked over the edge of the door. "There you are. Just checking to make sure my assigned list is here." She made a check on her paper. "You okay?"

Ula nodded, blinking. Tears leaked from the corners of her eyes.

The teasing she got, growing up as a preacher's kid, should have prepared her for this. Everyone must think she was a suitcase-lard-can-carrying baby. The self-pity helped wash the dural out of her eyes.

The excitement over, everyone went back to their jobs. Actually, very few had even stopped. Sniffing and wiping her nose, Ula climbed out of the bomb bay. To hell with them. All of them. They could think whatever they wanted. She wasn't here for them. She was doing this for Joe.

She tied wiring until the quitting whistle blew, ignoring the metal shavings itching their way down her collar and working into her bra and skin.

Cleaning Up

By the end of her work week, Ula's muscles had stiffened into boards. When the quitting whistle blew at one a.m., she shuffled toward the time clock. Gray-haired women passed her like marathon runners. The trio of redheaded women, known as The Reds, walked by, acknowledging her with, "You need a horse to get you there, Hillbilly?"

She stopped at the restroom. Women stood around the big circular stone sink, lathering their arms up to their elbows. Others removed pin curls that had been covered by bandanas, styling their hair for a night on the town.

Ula stared in the mirror. Patches of her face were pale, other parts oily and smudged with black grease, her cheeks sunken and eyes heavy-lidded. Tiny metal shavings dotted her hair. Grime covered her hands and arms, leaving trails of brown particles sliding toward the drain as she washed. White dust ringed her knees and the seat of her coveralls. A two-inch rip accented the left side, where she'd snagged the head of a bolt as she scooched across flooring. She hobbled away, leaving the chatter of the restroom. She rubbed the tension from her jaws, which she'd clenched each time she'd gripped a drill and forced it through metal.

Mina was waiting for her at the outer gates, licking an ice cream cone. "Peg, Big Mae, and I usually celebrate on payday; you don't look like you're gonna make it." Ula shook her head, staring at the *Closed* sign on Bill's Sweets wagon. With the limited production of ice cream, she should've gotten there early if she wanted one.

"My folks have Hildy, a Jersey cow." Ula put a hand on the concrete bench, lowering her body gradually, trying not to

135

groan. She stared across the night as though she could see the barn. "They have all the milk and butter they want. Even give it away."

"Wanna lick?" Mina held out the cone. Ula shook her head. "Well, you should treat yourself. There was a girl at our station who quit after an hour today. You made it a week. Celebrate!"

Ula surveyed the carts selling candy bars, hot dogs, coffee, and soda. She hadn't looked at her pay packet. She didn't want to be seen staring at it like some yokum who'd never seen a paycheck—which she hadn't. Whatever it was, it would have to stretch through the next week.

"Well, I'm making merry..." Mina pulled Ula up off the bench. "And we're having hot dogs—my treat. You're so thin, that uniform is falling off of you. How old are you, anyway?"

"Eighteen."

Mina gave her a look that rivaled the nuns'. Ula ignored her and got in line, watching The Reds, who somehow had gotten cones, after the shop was closed.

"How do you know your husband is in Sardinia?" Ula had learned the technique from her father. Even though he was a pastor, he kept all of his feelings, except anger, close to his chest. He was a champion at dropkicking emotional topics into someone else's court.

"We have a code. If Uncle Bill is ill, it means they were in a big battle. 'Glad the corn is growing,' means he's okay. He hates sardines—they're in that battle around Sardinia. Most everybody has a code."

Ula didn't. She didn't know where Kol was. Or poor Tommy. Or Joe. She'd have to go back through Joe's letters. She'd kept them all; maybe there were hints. Tommy had only written about the bombs and crying. Kol—he hadn't written at all. But how could he—he didn't know where she was.

Mina handed her a red and white paper tray holding a relish-onion-topped hot dog and turned to spoon condiments onto hers. "So you came all the way from Oklahoma by your-self?"

Ula nodded, pretending she hadn't noticed that the conversation had been spiked back to her.

Mina gave Ula a knowing look. "That's pretty brave for someone so young."

"How long have you been married?" It was a weak lob across the emotional net, but it was all Ula had.

"Seven months. Spur of the moment thing. We dashed to the courthouse and got hitched. They're open all night here. A janitor and another couple we didn't even know were our witnesses. George shipped out the next morning."

Ula looked away, blinking.

"You okay? What's the matter?" Mina leaned forward to look at her.

Ula pushed away a tear. "The onions are hot."

At 2:30 a.m., the windows of Mrs. Bell's house were bright with light. The ladies moved between rooms, getting ready for their night on the town. Mrs. Bell followed, snapping off lamps, timidly citing expenses and Civil Defense rules.

In her room, Ula stepped out of her coveralls.

"Good Lord!" Big Mae stopped pulling off her heavy jeans and stared. "Were you in a fight with a truck?"

Ula shook her head, hurriedly slipping into her thin cotton robe. Usually she changed in the bathroom, but Peg was hogging it. Big Mae, without a wisp of self-consciousness, continued shucking out of her shirt and long handles. "How'd you get it?" She glanced up, expecting an answer.

"A guy dropped a wrench on me. It actually looks better now."

Big Mae crossed the room in her bra and tugged Ula's robe from her shoulder. The deep purple splotch was tinted with reds, the edges petering into a sickly yellow. "Well, I hope you clobbered the son-of-a-bitch with that wrench several times."

"It was an accident." Ula leaned away, dragging her robe from Big Mae's grasp.

"Listen. I weld at the bottom of a thirty-foot hold. It's blacker than a witch's butt crack in there and just as cold. Men working above me used to drop tools, belts, hot rivets. Hell, they didn't care. They didn't like working with women. Of course, I can't hear a thing; it's so damn loud, I can scream while I weld and not even hear myself. Every bang of the riveters and screech of the chippers bounces back and forth against those metal walls. One day a drill—a drill with a half-inch bit—glances off the side of my welding mask. A whole damn drill, trailing twenty feet of cord! It broke my light. It could've split my head open.

"So I climb up the ladders—in the dark. And when this guy thanks me and reaches to take his drill. I walloped him with it about four times and left him hog-tied with the electrical cord. You know what? Since then, if anyone works above me, they make damn sure their tools are attached. And several women have thanked me."

Mina, in her bathrobe, leaned against the doorway. "I see you're getting the Don't-Put-Up-With-That Lecture. We've all heard it. My rule is...the first time anyone gives you crap—ignore it. The second time—talk tough. The third time? Then you do a Big Mae on 'em."

"Come here, Meeny. Look at this." Big Mae pulled Ula's gown off her shoulder again.

Mina inspected the small, red bumps across Ula's back, pulling the gown from the other shoulder. "Termites."

"What? I'm talking about this bruise the size of a cat's leg."

"You've even got them across your front." Mina pulled the robe down farther. Ula grabbed at her chest, trying to keep her bosom covered—even though she wore a bra. "Peg!" Mina called. "Get out of the bathroom. Ula needs an Epsom salts bath."

"What is it?" Big Mae poked at the rash-like bumps, speaking over whatever Ula was trying to say.

"We call it dural termites. Slivers of aluminum work under the skin. I'm surprised it's not itching like crazy."

"I'll roust Peg and start the bathwater." Big Mae wrapped a dressing gown around her and left.

Ula slumped onto the bed, pulling her robe back to her shoulders, staring at the floor. Mina sat beside her. Neither spoke.

From the hallway, Lindell's voice whined, "I'm gonna tell Ma. You're only supposed to use two inches of water."

"Get to bed, you little bird turd," Big Mae called.

Footsteps ran the other way, followed by the galloping clomp of Big Mae in pursuit. The sound of water filling the tub continued.

"Why didn't you say something?" Mina asked.

Ula looked up, blinking back tears, her hands fiddling with the tie on her robe. "I'm trying to be more *adult*. Take care of myself. I keep failing. I need to learn how to stand on my own."

"Oh, Ula." Mina started to put her arm around the girl's shoulders then hesitated and patted her knee instead. "Hasn't anyone ever told you we're *each* our brother's keeper?"

Ula wiped her eyes with her robe belt. "My father."

"Well, he was right. Let's get you into that bath." She pulled her to her feet. "Keep your shoulders under the hot water. It'll draw out the redness and the metal."

Peg appeared and took Ula's other arm. "And be very gentle with your washcloth."

"Oh, let her get in and splash to her heart's content," Big Mae huffed as she topped the stair landing and followed them to the bathroom.

In spite of Ula's protests, they removed her robe and held her arms as she stepped into the tub. "Okay. Okay. I can bathe myself." She tried to hit each one with a scowl, but her stare hung up, and she let out a gasp.

Big Mae charged the door where a head disappeared from view. "Get to bed, you little shit." The thunder of feet trampled down the stairs.

Peg and Mina left, shutting the door behind them, but the hushed whisper of their voices came from the hallway, including Mrs. Bell's mumblings about San Diego's wartime water shortage.

Ula sank, submerging her shoulders in the luxury of hot water. She splashed her face then let out a long breath, her gaze finally settling on the bathroom window. Outside, it was dark, which surprised her, because inside, she felt the smallest ember of hope. Just a flicker. And the sense that a prayer was being answered. A prayer prayed by someone else.

Instead of partying, she'd gone to bed and was up early the next morning for their half-day off. The household usually didn't awaken until eleven, except for Mrs. Bell, who was supposed to get Lindell to school by eight. Half the time he stayed home, complaining he needed more sleep. Mrs. Bell didn't seem to mind.

Ula moved slowly, mostly because she was sore, but also because the old house creaked reconnaissance reports of her location.

It tattled that someone else was up, too, and before Ula was able to duck out, Mina caught her in the kitchen. "Where're you going?"

"A quick trip to the bank. I need to cash my check." Ula stuffed the rest of her oleo sandwich in her mouth as she headed toward the door.

"Good. I'll go with you."

"I'd rather do it by myself." Ula cast a sullen glance at her which flashed into surprise. Her roommate had transformed into a different woman. Prettier. Her brown hair rolled over her ears. She wore make-up, a blue-striped dress, and a periwinkle-blue hat framing her face in a semi-circle.

"I won't slow you down. Let's go. Got a purse?" Mina opened the door. Ula shook her head. "What're you putting your money in?"

"My shoe." They both looked down at her well-worn, round-toed frogskins.

They walked six blocks to the thoroughfare, making small talk about the wisps of fog that hadn't burned off yet. When they'd cashed their checks and came out of the bank, people were standing in front of Bealle's Grocery.

Mina tugged Ula into the line. She asked the narrow-faced woman in front of her, "What are we waiting for?"

"I don't know." The woman spoke rapidly, her words full of excitement. "Rationing causes me to get into a line whenever I see one. It's bound to be something I need."

"Isn't that the truth?" Mina agreed. "I hope it's soap." She inspected Ula. "Even with the shortage, we've got to find you some. Your face is breaking out like a teenager's." The woman in front of them turned to appraise Ula too.

"I hate lines," Ula mumbled and turned away. She felt like a kid the moment before entering church; sure that these women were going lick their hankies and rub a smudge from her face.

It turned out the grocery had received a shipment of bananas. People acted as though Christmas had come in October, each clutching their allowed two pieces of fruit.

"I'm going to the drugstore. I need another uniform. And I'm doing it alone," Ula declared.

"Just remember to save enough for rent. You'll need breakfast and lunch food for the week too. And buy a pail, so you can scrap that lard can." Mina lifted the fruit from Ula's hands. "I'll hide the 'naners from Lindell. We'll make bread for everybody, okay?"

Ula gave her a Novice's obedient smile and nodded. She waited, watching Mina walk several blocks, turn the corner and disappear. It was a gray day, but the smell of hibiscus growing in the temperate clime cheered her. She took a big breath of freedom, her arms wide. The first woman who walked by she asked, "Where's the nearest shoe store?"

Her new, strappy platforms were Hollywood red. She looked down as she walked, watching the peep-toes stride forward with each step. Next pay check, she'd get polish for her toenails. The heel height made her feel as though she were walking on tiptoe for six blocks. A tiny raw spot rubbed on the side of her foot, but that was the price of new shoes.

"Where is everyone?" She asked Mrs. Bell when she arrived with her packages.

"Big Mae is teaching Lindell how to throw a baseball. Mina is tending the Victory garden, and Peg is at the USO Club."

Ula looked through the window into the back yard. Big Mae had Lindell so riled, he was trying to bean her with the baseball.

"That's it," the husky woman yelled. "Now you're finally throwin' some heat with your little chicken wing." When Big Mae tossed the ball, Lindell usually missed it, ignoring the woman's shouts, "Put your body in front of it, ya little twig." He'd watch it bounce into the squash vines or spinach greens, his hands quivering in front of him like a beggar asking for alms. Mina made him lift leaves and get it himself, telling him the slugs wouldn't bite.

Turning from the window, Ula took money out of her old frogskins in the shoebox. "I'm curious. Why Lindell isn't in school today?" She counted out five dollars and pushed the cash toward her landlady.

Without looking at her, Mrs. Bell stuffed it in the pocket of her apron. "He's been rather delicate since his father died."

The front door opened and closed, but the women ignored it. Both stared into the backyard as though checking the boy's frail condition. Big Mae popped the kid with a baseball, telling him, "See. That didn't hurt as much as you thought." Ula doubted the ten-year-old would remain a sissy with Big Mae around, but all she said to Mrs. Bell was, "I'm sorry about your husband."

She pulled another Consolidated Vultee blue uniform and red bandana from a box, along with a bag of Epsom salts to replace Peg's. She'd planned on splurging on feminine hygiene pads, but they were wildly expensive—with most of the cotton going to produce bandages. As it was, she hadn't been able to buy much food.

Peg came into the kitchen, humming and dancing. "You'll never believe who I met this time, ladies!" she gushed. Mrs. Bell and Ula gave each other long-suffering looks. "Oh! Snazzy shoes!" She pointed at Ula's feet. "You have to take them jitterbugging." Without waiting for a response, she launched into a breathless story of Clark Gable joking with the soldiers at the USO club while Marlene Dietrich waited tables like a regular girl.

After nine weeks, Ula had a routine. Up at eleven o'clock, she'd have toast and write a letter, rotating between Joe, Tommy, her Mom, or the Sisters of the Holy Trail. The notes to Tommy were the hardest. Now that she understood his terror, what could she say to soothe him? If she thought about him too much, panic exploded in her heart, multiplying fears for her brother.

She wrote of simple homefront news: dimouts, long work hours, funny stories. She always added, "I'm praying for you." It wasn't enough.

To the nuns, she put two dollars in an envelope, asking that they send her some lye soap. Since it could take off skin, she was sure it would remove airplane grease.

At one o'clock, she ate a lunch of boiled eggs and whatever vegetables she could glean from the spring garden. Her extra time went into sewing or reading. All of the ladies left at three to catch a bus for work. Big Mae, who started an hour later than the others, liked to arrive at the shipyard early and "suit up," donning several pairs of heavy pants, wool underwear, flannel shirts, three pairs of socks, and her welder's apron and mask, explaining, "Those docks are colder than a tin toilet seat."

Ula liked to arrive early, too, leaving Mina gabbing at the outer gate. As soon as she clocked in, she'd go to one of the Day Shift's ships to pirate hidden motors and parts.

"Whad'ja find?"

The gruff voice made Ula drop the floor board she was peeking under. She scowled at the big man. "Why do you sneak up on people like that?" She lifted the flooring again and pulled out a drill—a sure sign it was good equipment, not one that got hot or shocked the user.

"That's why they call me Gator. Can't help it you're so jumpy." He watched Ula load herself with a confiscated ladder, lamp, and drill, looping an electrical cord over her shoulder. "So when we goin' out?"

"We're not. Excuse me." She tried to get past, but he stepped forward, his bulk pinning her against metal framing. The starting whistle blew throughout the plant, matching the alarms in Ula's head. Gator didn't move.

"You forgot. I've been keepin' your secret about sleepin' on the job. If I said one word, you woulda been fired. Just like that." He pistol-pointed his finger and shot it at her; then he bent closer, inches from her face. "You owe me, doll."

Ula exploded like a crazy woman, screaming the pipefitters' favorite swear words and slinging her arms to get enough space to swing the drill at his head. She'd only meant to growl a little tough talk, but this job was hard on her religion. Uncooperative wires and pipes that had to be forced into impossibly tiny spaces. Banged-up shins, elbows, and shoulders. Big, sleazy idiots like this sack of sloth. The profanity she'd bitten back for weeks spewed forth.

Gator's eyebrows raised.

"Lord have mercy!" A man's slow drawl came from the doorway. "Who woulda thought that?" Skinny Delbert ambled forward. "I haven't heard cussin' like that since...well, I've actually never heard anything like that from a lady. Here, lemme help you, Ula." He reached for her equipment. "Move back, Gator."

The big man shifted to avoid getting a face full of the electrical cord Delbert swung over his shoulder. The ladder fumbled to the floor, barely missing Gator's foot and moving him back another step. Ula hurried for the door. Delbert followed, giving Gator a slow grin. "Well, I got what I came for. Hope the rest of your shift is quieter."

Gator nodded with a sidelong look, his eyes not sharing the wide smile he flashed.

"Damn Red Button sent me to find you." Delbert studied Ula as he dropped the equipment inside the Swing Shift's ship. "He wants to see you."

"Why?"

Delbert shrugged. "You okay? Where'd you learn to cuss like that?"

"Another life. Are we working tubes together tonight?" He nodded. "Then you start I'll go see what Mr. Dillard wants."

"Ula." He grabbed her arm, lowering his voice as others entered the fuselage. "Tell Dillard about Gator. He won't stand for such nonsense."

"You're sweet." She touched his fingers before sliding from his grip. "But you know how a stool pigeon is treated around here. And I'm stupid. I should've waited. The start whistle had sounded. People would've been coming on board and scared him away. I'm sorry you had to hear that. Anyhow...I'm sure he got the message...I'm not looking for a boyfriend."

Delbert watched her hurry down the tail chute. He sat on his tool box, picked up a pipe, staring at the fitting. "Yeah," he said, "I got the message."

One of the gray-haired women, delivering switches to the bomb bay, patted his back as she passed.

Ula found Mr. Dillard at the Station 18 work table.

"Li'l Okie, you been here how long?"

"Over two months, sir."

"And now you're training other gals. I told you, you could do it. A foreman can tell how hard a gal works by how dirty she gets, and you're usually grimy from head to toe. Here's something to put in your toolbox."

Ula took the thick safety glasses with a smile that said they were eight weeks too late. She'd mastered the art of dodging dural.

"And...now you need to go buy your own tools."

"I can't afford—"

He held up a hand, staving off protests and scribbled a list on a sheet of paper. "I've let you slide too long. Go to the company store and get these. You'll thank me someday. Good tools last forever if you take care of 'em."

At the top of the list was *Toolbox.*

"Thanks. I love to spend what little money I have on things I don't need." Ula whapped the safety glasses against the wooden workbench as she left. She made the quarter mile trek to the plant's tool store, stomping part of the way. While waiting to be helped, she studied a poster of a young woman sitting on her toolbox having lunch. *Good Job, Sister!* the words proclaimed. *We Never Figured You Could Do A Man-Sized Job. America's Women Have Met the Test!* Something about the poster irked her.

She purchased only half the tools on the list. Payments would be deducted from her check each week. "It's a good beginning," Mr. Dillard told her when she returned and crabbily showed him. "Women need a tool chest as well as men. Money well spent. You'll be doing three ships a morning if you don't have to hunt down tools."

"Pffft! I don't see how this helps. Even with my tool-gathering, I'm more productive than men like Dan and Gator. Their tool boxes are open only in case you stick your head in the ship. They're too busy playing cards to need tools."

She carefully latched her metal box. "You still want me to do tube installations tonight?"

Mr. Dillard was gone, walking toward the ship, his face dark as a thundercloud. Ula groaned. She'd meant to show the toolbox was unnecessary, not to squeal on fellow workers. Surely, Mr. Dillard knew of the warning system. Whoever worked near an opening called out "Red Button"—the badge all foremen wore. By the time the boss stuck his head in the ship, everyone was busy as though they lived to do their jobs.

Ula didn't follow him. People might connect her to Mr. Dillard's fury. She walked to the nose as though she had a job to do. Climbing the platform, she felt the tool box banging her shins on each rung. It would be safe in the fore. Dan and Gator stayed in the tail, stuffing just enough cables under the floor to make it look as though they'd done some work.

Stepping onto the platform landing, Ula saw both men sitting on the floor of the empty command deck. The fore crew had finished and moved to the next plane. "Nuts, nuts, *nuts!*" She growled the last word.

Ula's clanking approach up the stairs and mild profanity had distracted the pair. They'd missed the early signal of Mr. Dillard's entry from the tail. A voice saying, "They're up there," was their only warning. They barely had time to toss their cards in their boxes and slam the lids.

Mr. Dillard burst into the cabin, catching them without tools, sitting, and staring at each other. "Both of you!" The foreman pointed. "What've you done today?"

Ula backed down the ladder. Gator's glare locked on her. His eyes narrowed as though he aimed a shotgun.

Meringue Charm School

"Let's go to that charm program today," Ula begged, looking over her shoulder. "I don't want to hang around here."

"I don't need any charm. I'm already married." Mina opened her lunch pail.

Ula slammed it shut and took off with it, forcing Mina to follow. As they walked to the Building 4 Meeting Room, Ula told her about Gator's romantic threats and how she'd accidentally ratted him out for something completely different.

Mina groaned. "You little ninny. Think before you open your mouth."

"Big Mae doesn't."

"She's husky enough to get away with it. How will hiding cut help? Are you charming him into forgiveness?"

Ula pushed Mina through the door, where the elegant, slim-skirted Mrs. Oakmont gave them a gracious smile and waved toward wooden chairs as she continued her lecture.

"...and I told my husband as we sat at the restaurant, 'I can always tell an aircraft worker.' They have an "S" slouch. Their shoulders and chest bend forward, their tail end dragging behind. Sit up ladies. Straighten your spines." Women shuffled in their chairs, correcting their posture.

Mina rolled her eyes, opened her lunch pail, and pulled out her Spam sandwich. Ula looked around; a few others were eating, so she ate too. Mrs. Oakmont walked back and forth in front of the group, balancing a book on her head. It made Ula remember posture-correct piano practices with five minutes added each time the book fell off her head.

149

"Freshen up your lipstick several times a day." Mrs. Oakmont held up the gold tube. "Grace in everything you do, ladies. You can be refined in the way you speak and handle a drill, or you can act like a gorilla." She mugged a face, acting as though she were punching a drill through a wall like it was a battering ram. Women laughed.

"Oh, brother," Mina mumbled. "There's nothin' in that pie, but meringue. I bet she's never held a drill in her life."

"Do you have a question?" Mrs. Oakmont walked over to Mina as the laughter faded.

"Actually, yes, I do." Mina sat up. "This has plagued me ever since I've worked here." She tossed the crusts of her sandwich in her pail as she spoke. "I often have to make an overhead installation, and I can't use a ladder. The only way I can get to it is to straddle the hatch entrance, balancing one foot on each hand railing. Of course, people come and go between my legs. How do you suggest I do that gracefully?"

"My!" Mrs. Oakmont tapped her chin. "I'd ask Engineering to create a ladder-device for me, so I could do my job safely." Several women laughed. "Ladies." She gave them a silencing look. "Remember, most matters of grace can be solved by keeping your feet together." Smoothly lowering into a chair, she made an exaggerated show of turning her legs slightly to the side and crossing her ankles. "But in your case..." she nodded toward Mina "...I'd say get a special ladder and try to keep your knees together."

She held up a carton, her voice full of excitement. "Now, that completes our time. I have wonderful samples from Dorothy Gray Cosmetics."

Mina applied her tiny tube of Apple Red lipstick as they walked back to their stations. "This is the only reason to go to that farce. I wonder if the samples will be different next week."

"What should I do about Dan and Gator?" Ula stuffed her tube in her pocket.

"Stop fretting. They don't know it was you. Mr. Dillard accused them of slacking, not bothering you. Stay out of their way. And if that doesn't work, put on your lipstick and charm them. Just remember to keep your ankles crossed."

The afternoon went smoothly. Ula strung the electric wires that made bombs drop. Rumors grumbled through the ship when Dan was spotted out on the wing, holding a bucking bar for a riveter. It was usually an entry-level job for a woman, but he braced the backside of the sheet metal as a gal punched a rivet through. "The Union will put a stop to that," a man groused. Others whispered it had been long overdue. Ula said nothing—until Gator came into her area with the black stuff.

She was on top of a ladder, screwdriver in one hand, screws in the other, securing a metal cover plate over a switch. The section was emptying of workers. Black stuff had that effect. Ula breathed through her mouth and tried to hurry as Gator squeezed the gooey, synthetic rubber around self-sealing gas tanks. She wondered how anything so foul smelling—a combo of rotten eggs and garbage dump—was supposed to absorb leaking fuel if the tanks were hit during a combat mission. Surely, gasoline improved the odor.

"I know it was you." Gator thumped the bottom of her ladder with his foot. "I could see it in your face, the moment that damn Dillard walked in."

"I don't know what you're talking about." She twisted screws as fast as she could. Her legs told her to jump and run. Her head scolded her to stay. Had Joe been making a bomb run and the doors wouldn't open because some girl had been frightened and hadn't finished the job?

"I'll remember." Gator kicked the ladder again. Ula frantically cranked on the last screw. The screwdriver flipped out of her hand.

"Whoops!" Gator bent over, picked it up, and handed it back to her.

"Thank you." She took it without looking at him. Three more twists, and the job was finished. She hopped down, stooping to close her tool box.

The top tray of tools was covered in black stuff.

"Whoops." He shrugged again and turned back to the gas tanks.

"You jackass!" Ula shrieked. "It's not even paid for."

"I had rubber gloves that came up to my armpits, and I scrubbed with yellow, gaggy solvent." Ula stood at Mrs. Bell's stove, frying meat in the biggest cast iron skillet she had. They'd combined ration stamps for their monthly liver and onion feast. Mrs. Bell and Lindell hated the taste and smell. They'd sequestered themselves upstairs with knitting and a Marvel Mystery comic book. Ula took over head-cook duties because of her convent-kitchen training. "Mr. Dillard ordered Dan and Gator to help, but I didn't want to be near them."

Peg mumbled around a toothpick sticking from her mouth, which was supposed to keep her from tearing as she sliced onions. "Mayee he leave you 'lone, now he hav revenge." She raked the slices into the skillet.

"Any jackrat harasses me, I strike an arc. They don't come close." Big Mae slid plates and silverware around the table then plopped in a chair.

"Well, Ula doesn't carry a welder." Steam rolled into air as Mina dumped boiled cauliflower and carrots into a bowl. "So that's no help."

"Got a crescent wrench?" Big Mae asked. Ula shook her head. "It's a dandy tool, and you can stick it in your butt pocket. Each time this Gator guy comes near, you whip it out and threaten to tighten his nuts if he gets any closer."

The women stared at her for several seconds. The meat and onions sizzled and popped. Peg burst into giggles. "I can hardly see our sweet, young Ula doing that."

"It's all in how you say it. Try it Ula."

Ula gave a half-hearted attempt, shaking her spatula at Big Mae.

"No!" Peg exclaimed. "Like this." She jabbed her knife, growling like a pirate, "If you come any closer, I'll tighten your nuts." Laughter echoed through the kitchen as Ula set the meat on the table, steam curling from the caramelized onions.

"This is the kind of charm school they should teach at Consolidated." Mina said as she spackled a pat of oleo on top of the vegetables. "I'd go every week if they'd throw in free makeup."

"Which reminds me..." Peg scooted her chair in. "Ula, you need to take your new lipstick and shoes dancing with us."

"Don't encourage her, Peg. I don't think she even takes those shoes off to sleep." Big Mae shook a fork at Ula. "You're already ruining your feet. It's not natural, squeezing your toes together. You can't dance in those stilts."

"I could do cartwheels in these beauties." Ula waggled a platform wedgie in the air.

"When you learn to tell off Gator without giggling like a school girl," Big Mae said, "I'll let you go boogie-woogin with us." As they passed the liver around the table, each woman practiced saying, "I'll tighten your nuts," and grunting other threats that had the punch of snowflakes.

Ula tried to buy a crescent wrench at the company store the next day. "We don't have one. That's forged steel. Don't you know there's a war on?" She was sick of hearing that. She settled on a one-inch box end wrench, the longest tool she could find, figuring it would extend her reach.

By the following week, Gator had warned everyone at Station 18 to watch their back when Ula was around. The few friends she'd made didn't want to eat with her.

Mina surprised her by finding her for lunch. "C'mon, let's go to Mrs. Snooty's charm class. I hear they have new samples."

Ula was staring out the window of the meeting room when a volunteer was requested. Mina's hand shot up, her elbow grazing Ula's head. She was walking toward the front before Ula could rub it. Mrs. Oakmont dipped her polished nails into a jar of cold cream and rubbed a small white spot on Mina's face. "Now all she has to do is relax and read a magazine for a few minutes." Everyone laughed. "None of that soap and water business which will dry your skin."

Using a white wash cloth, the matron wiped away cream and displayed the gray grime on the cloth. "And feel how lovely your skin is." Mina followed orders, rubbing and ooohing at the baby-bottom softness. "This is for you—for volunteering." She handed Mina a whole jar and continued listing the benefits of cold cream: a lip protector, a sun burn ointment, a face mask...

As they filed out the door, Mina whispered, "My friend on the Night Shift told me to volunteer. This stuff is expensive." Ula looked at the tiny sample packet she was given. "I'll show you what you really use this goop for." Mina stopped at the restroom, instructing Ula to wash her hands and arms. "Now slather your cream on them. Ula only had enough for one arm. "That's it. Don't wash it off until quitting time."

Ula went back to work, poking her white arm. It didn't feel any different—just greasier than usual. Climbing the ladder, she was horrified to discover the ship was "in the paint."

The Reds sashayed onto the ship. Their flame-haired leader, Bab, paused, watching Ula drill holes in the flooring. "Heard you're a snitch." She pulled off her snood and put on a green turban. The other three red-heads did the same, chattering as they pushed every strand of their hair under the fabric. Bab reapplied her lipstick then clapped the lid on, still staring at Ula. "Way to go, Yeehaw."

In the past weeks, Bab had shortened her comments. All remarks about Okies and horse operas had stopped. She simply said, "Yeehaw," as she passed, adding a droll look.

The Reds fanned out, putting tape over the instructions or warnings on the fuselage walls and covering arrows on control boxes. They were surprisingly efficient and fast, even though they yammered across the ship the entire time and often stopped to reapply their lipstick. Small towels hung from their back pockets. They wiped their hands and arms frequently. They carried cardboard and newspapers with them, never sitting on dust and metal shavings on the floor.

"Move," said one of the ladies as she stepped over Ula sitting on the floor.

Ula made her wait until she'd rubbed Vaseline on the connections and tightened the screw brackets. The moment she leaned back, the woman leaned in, taping paper over the wiring box she'd just completed.

"The painters are here," Bab announced. "You done, Yeehaw? Or has all that snitchin' put you behind?"

Ula tossed her needle nose pliers and screwdriver into her box, slammed the lid, and stood, inches from Bab's down-turned face.

"Look. To my knowledge, I've never said anything negative to you or about you. I ignore what you say because I've got a brother who's probably rotting away in a POW camp. You and your girls may act like snobs, but you don't mess around. I respect that. I have no sentiment for jackasses who just pretend to work. The more planes we get out there, the sooner my brother comes home. So I'd appreciate it if you'd stop giving me crap."

Ula didn't wait for an answer, she mumbled, "Excuse me," and worked her way out the door. Without looking back, she climbed into the next Swing Shift ship. Several other workers followed her. The Reds left, too, none of them chatting. As soon as everyone had jounced down the ladder, the painters moved in, spraying the bomb bay the color of a gray day.

The air inside and outside of the ship became foggy, paint covering the cables, brackets, and harsh words that still hung there. Everything would blend into one dismal, overcast color—appropriate for a weapon of war.

When the quitting whistle blew four hours later, Ula hurried to the bathroom to tell Mina what had happened—but she couldn't. The Reds entered, taking down their hair, styling it in rolls, adding bobby pins topped with fabric flowers.

"Look! Look at my arm." Mina held it out. "Notice how clean it is."

"Nice." Ula nodded, watching the Reds as she touched the wrench in her back pocket, hoping she never had to threaten anyone with it.

"Wash your arm!" Mina yanked Ula's hand beneath the spray of water in the circular sink. "Just add a little soap...and see..."

Several women came over to look. Where the cold cream had been was clean. No black grime lodged in the pores. No scrubbing.

The experiment brought a slew of questions from women. "How much did you use?" "But it's so expensive." "Look it keeps gunk from under the nails too."

Bab caught Ula's eyes. The redhead gave her a single nod. Ula returned it.

As they left the plant, Ula was sure of two things: The drugstore was going to double their cold cream sales today. And cleaning up dirty situations was more about what she revealed than what she tried to cover up.

"They're perfect." Peg stood in the kitchen admiring the lines she'd drawn down the back of her roommates' legs, using an eyebrow pencil. "Turn around."

Big Mae and Ula faced her. Mina looked up from her *Ladies Home Journal.* "Big Mae looks splotchy."

"Damn!" The large woman moved to the table. "I don't see why I have to wear leg make up. I shaved."

"You did? Really? Well, until they make nylons instead of parachutes, you'll have to use leg-make up. And don't mess up the seam I drew." Peg moved around the kitchen fastening hooks, straightening bows in hair. "Mrs. Bell, I believe some tea would calm us. Could you put on the kettle?"

"A Seagram's and Seven-Up would be better." Big Mae smirked as she rubbed flesh-colored cream onto her calf.

Ula did a little Lindy Hop in her strappy platforms. "I'm going to dance all evening."

"You've only got a half-day off. We need to leave for work at seven," Mina said flatly.

"Go with us. It's a group date. Guys from my work. We're not pairing off. You're turning into a dull old woman." Peg tugged at Mina's magazine.

"What part of married do you not get?" She yanked it back.

The doorbell rang, sending the women into a flutter of voices. Footsteps thudded down the stairs, two at a leap.

"Lindell!" Peg shouted. "Get back to your room!" She turned to her landlady, urgency in her voice. "Would you see he's upstairs before answering the door?" She faced Ula and Big Mae. "We're not going to charge the guys like a herd of elephants. We're just in the kitchen having a cup of tea. Ho-hum. Oh, it's time to go? We didn't realize."

Mrs. Bell's footsteps thumped across the wooden floor, followed by a scream. She ran back into the kitchen. "There's a man in a uniform at the door. Oh Lord. Oh Lord. Not again. He's bringing the notice."

"Mrs. Bell!" Peg shook her. "Your husband's gone. It can't be for you."

"It doesn't matter." The whites of Mrs. Bell's eyes were big. "Bad news is outside that door."

"No." Mina's face turned to stone. "No. I haven't heard from George in weeks. I won't answer it. I won't go." A tense silence bounced around the kitchen.

"All right." Big Mae stood, straightening her skirt. "I have no one to lose. I'll go."

The house echoed with the heavy tread of her feet. The door hinges squeaked, followed by muffled voices. Big Mae called from the living room, "Ula."

Ula felt a cold shroud envelop her. The finger of death had swung in her direction. They must've found Joe. Her mother must have told them to notify her since she was so close to the naval base. Slowly, she stood. Hands patted her shoulder. Mrs. Bell still clung to Peg.

She took a breath then walked toward the front door, hearing the others shuffle to peek from the kitchen. Big Mae stepped aside, revealing a handsome man in a heavy wool coat. Two rows of gold buttons adorned the front. He held a white hat in gloved hands.

"Kol?" Ula whispered.

Shoe Repair Needed

Big Mae moved aside, her eyes flashing wide and a concerned twist to her lips.

Kol stepped inside. The women in the kitchen crowded the doorway for a better look.

With a *Thud! Thud!* Lindell made it down the stairs in two jumps, crashing onto the floor between Ula and Kol. He hopped up, shaking a hammer and bellowing from the bottom of his lungs, "Don't get any closer or I'll tighten your nuts!"

"Oh for Pete's sake!" Big Mae grabbed at him. "Give it here, you little shit."

Kol grinned at the boy. "I have no doubt you plan to do some damage with that." Lindell jabbed the hammer at him like it was a sword. "You the man of the house, buddy? Protecting these women?"

Lindell puffed up and gave a nod.

"Then I ask permission to come aboard. I'd like to talk to this one." He pointed at Ula.

"If she's your date, then I'm warning you...she twists ears."

"Yeah, she's twisted my ears a few times. Can I sit over there and talk to her?"

With vee fingers, the boy drew a line between his eyes and Kol's. "Okay, but I'm watchin' you."

"No, you aren't." Irritation underlined Ula's voice. "Kol, this is Lindell, and these are my roommates..." As Ula named them and pointed, they waved. "Ladies, this is...this is Captain Kol Kellner of the Merchant Marine."

"All right, we'd best get going." Big Mae gave a single clap, rubbing her hands together. "Grab your jackets. It looks like it might rain. We'll just step outside—"

The doorbell rang again.

Lindell jumped forward, waving his hammer and growling.

"Wait, bud. Hold on a minute." Kol held up a hand. "Let's you and me do this together." Lindell nodded as Kol opened the door and stepped onto the porch to greet a group of young men. "I assume all of you will act like gentlemen this evening, if not, my first mate will take care of you. He nudged Lindell, whispering, "Now."

The boy shook the hammer, screaming from the porch steps. "I will tighten your nuts!"

"Well said." Kol nodded and called through the door, "Ladies...your dates."

His eyes locked with Ula's. They stared at each other a moment, then Ula let out a huff and walked to the couch instead of outside. Kol joined her. Mrs. Bell took the opportunity to grab Lindell and herd him up the stairs.

"That's quite a good-looking friend," Peg whispered, closing the front door as they left. "We should've invited them to go with us."

"No." Big Mae walked straight ahead without looking back. "When I answered the door, he identified himself as her husband."

"Here." Kol pulled a small rectangle wrapped in brown paper and tied with twine from his inner pocket.

Even through the paper, Ula could smell the undeniable scent of lye soap. "I should've known the nuns would tell you where I was. I didn't rat on you; they think you're wonderful. I figured you needed somewhere to go when you came to port. I said I was leaving to end the war faster. I didn't want them to know I was so stupid that I *thought* we were married and that you didn't bother to set me straight."

"I told them the whole of it. You should've seen Sister Heavé's face. Damnation never looked so fierce."

"You deserve it." She turned the bar over and over in her hand. "Why'd you do it? Why'd you take me from my home and ruin me? That's the part that hurt the worst."

"That wasn't my intent. Still isn't. I'm living in stolen moments with you, Ula. The rest of the time I'm transporting men, jeeps, and supplies as fast as possible to wherever they're needed. As soon as we dock, I usually have less than twenty-four hours before I leave."

"Don't give me that. There was time to get to a Justice of the Peace. I'm a little smarter now than I was then." She crossed her arms over her chest.

"I can see that. You look different."

"I hope so. You like my shoes?" She held up a foot, twisting her ankle to show off painted toenails peeking from her strappy platform shoe.

"No."

"Well, I like them."

"Ula, I'm sorry. I only thought of myself. But I've never stopped loving you or thinking of you as my wife. Marry me now. Tonight, before I have to leave again." He pulled a small wooden box from inside his jacket and handed it to her.

Ula opened it to find a ring. Then closed it. "It's a little late. All I feel is shame. I couldn't go home. I couldn't face the nuns. And now I'll have to answer my roommates' questions."

"Then marry me. Let me make it right."

"I have a job. I make good money. No one tells me where I can go or what I can wear..." she displayed her shoe again. "I went from my father bossing me around to you telling me—"

"You never obeyed anything I told you...such as our agreement to leave a message when one of us left."

"You're not my husband. I don't have to do what you say."

"Ula, I'm hauling troops and cargo overseas. Every invasion, I'm in the thick of it. I'll probably not make port again for some time. Marry me now."

"I don't even know..." she shook her head, looking around, "if I love you anymore."

The sound of silence was deafening. Neither looked at the other.

After a minute, Kol stood and pulled a roll of money from his pocket. "It's everything I have."

"I can't take this."

"I still consider you my wife. I'm sorry that I'm not here to take care of you. Keep the ring too."

"Why're you doing this?" Ula stood. "Please don't try to force my hand like this."

"May I kiss you?"

"I don't think that's a good idea. We need to—"

He grabbed her and kissed her long and hard. When he let go, he put on his cap and walked to the door. "Listen to me for once; if you get scared, go home. Good bye, Ula."

The door closed behind him with a quiet *click*. She still hadn't moved.

"Go after him!" Mina stood in the kitchen doorway.

"You were listening?"

"You just sent a man to his death." Her voice was damning.

"No. You don't know Kol. He always lands on his feet."

"Because he had a purpose! Listen to me," Mina crossed the floor and grabbed Ula's arms. "He just gave you everything he owns. He knows where he's going, and I can tell...he doesn't expect to come back."

Ula stared out the window, still feeling the warmth of his lips on her mouth.

"What do you want from the man?" Mina gave her a hard shake. "Heaven help you!" She roughly let go of Ula, went to the door, opened it, and looked out. "He tracked you down. He confessed to the Sisters. He said he was sorry. He gave you a ring. He did everything he could to marry you tonight, except drag you by the hair down to the courthouse. And when you said no, he *still* gave you everything. You'll regret this the rest of your life. You just broke a man's heart and sent him out to die."

Ula stared, as the truth of the situation slowly moved across her face. She pushed past Mina onto the porch. "Kol?" Only the patter of raindrops answered. Bounding down the steps, she ran toward the main thoroughfare.

After three blocks the strap on her right shoe broke. She stumbled, skinning her hands and knees on the sidewalk. Picking up the shoe, she ran clopping up and down. He wasn't at the bus stop. Scanning the street, she didn't see him in any store entryway—out of the rain. The Bijou ticket taker said she hadn't seen him. According to Kathy, he hadn't been in the drugstore.

He was gone.

Ula leaned against the brick wall outside the diner, catching her reflection in the glass door. The rain had plastered her hair to her head. Dark mascara lines ran down her face. Her dress stuck to her body. Brown streaks of leg make-up ebbed toward her ankles.

"Hey, sister! How 'bout doing a little war work?"

She turned to see a Marine and his buddy grinning at her.

"Oh, go away. Please just go away and try to stay alive."

Damn, but she hated these hooker shoes.

Sharks On A Train

"I believe that's enough for tonight," Aunt Ula said as the train slowed to a stop. It took a moment for Matty to shake a rainy San Diego street from her thoughts. She looked out the window. "When did it get dark?"

The hooded lampposts of the Tucson Depot barely pushed the night away. Cool blues and purples of desert sky and stars crowded the edges of the station.

Aunt Ula arose, walking to the dining car. "Wait." Matty scrambled after her. "What did your roommates say? Did you ever see Kol again?

The concierge turned and led the women to a table when he saw them coming down the aisle. There were always a few people like this on every trip. They waited until the dining car was almost empty, then sauntered in and ordered, ensuring the staff would be there late, vacuuming and filling salt shakers rather than playing a few rounds of poker before they turned in. Usually, the late stragglers were men, not an unlikely pair like this old woman and a walking cover for *Rolling Stones*— the rodeo issue.

"I'm having Red Velvet cake," Aunt Ula said as she sat.

"I only have one pre-order ticket that was filled out at lunchtime: It's for Chicken Marsala. The concierge placed the form in front of her. "It's signed...Katherine Hepburn. Is that you madam?"

"It is." She pushed it aside. "I look different because I'm going through a rough patch called aging. I still want cake. Throw the chicken on the plate if that'll make you feel better."

"You've still retained your charm and wit over the years, Ms. Hepburn." He turned toward Matty. "And what would Rosalind Russell like?"

"I have no idea who that is." Matty gave him the look her Millennial generation used when someone's jokes were as funny as telephones with cords. "I'll have the tacos and a glass of wine."

"Wait." Aunt Ula grabbed the concierge's arm. "I'd like a Spanish coffee. It carries a fond memory for me. I need that tonight." The waiter nodded.

With elbows crossed and resting on the table, Matty leaned forward. "What happened next?"

"I've bent your ear all day, dear. We need to come back to the present for a while."

"At least tell me...you were glad to get away from the nuns, weren't you?"

Aunt Ula gave an iffy sideways nod. "Then—yes. Now, no. Did you know there's a crematorium in Portland, Oregon where six stories of the dead hang out?"

Matty frowned and squinted.

"The oldest, smallest rooms, way down in the basement, have marble floors and gilded metalwork from the 1800s. Shelf after shelf, floor to ceiling, they're full of metal books. Each person's ashes are contained in bronzed containers that look like books. Thousands of thick volumes. It's really something to ponder."

With a glance, she stilled Matty. "Hold on. I'll eventually get to a point. You see, that's who we are: bumping into strangers, helping or hindering each other into the next chapter of our story. So, without the nuns, how would I have made it through what came next? The Sisters weren't uncaring...I was young. I couldn't see any plot to my life. Still can't, but it's taken years for me to trust the Master Author—which is hilarious now that I think about it. The story has continued whether I participated willingly or dug my heels in and had to be pushed through the next part. The only difference was my rebellion."

A young waiter set their food and drinks in front of them.

Aunt Ula stuck a finger in the chocolate icing and licked it off. "Now, let's talk about kittens, or what to do when you toot in a crowd, or anything funny. It's best not to dig through the graves of the past when it's nighttime. I'm afraid the story turns rather dark from here. Best to dig up those bones in the daylight."

"It gets worse?" Matty frowned. "The war is already depressing."

"Things usually get worse before they get better." She shrugged. "I might even tell you the real reason I got on this train."

"It's not to go to the Lutheran Ladies Convention?"

"Drink. Eat. We'll sleep. Tomorrow's a new chapter." The cars lurched as they pulled from the depot. Matty wore the slight slant of a smile as she held up her glass. Aunt Ula clinked her coffee cup against it.

Below them, outside their window, squares of light flickered across sandy dirt. A rabbit dashed from the rails and hid in sagebrush as the monster's steel wheels turned.

The hare watched the chugging metal creature pick up speed and roar away into the darkness with its heartbeat strumming the air. After many miles and minutes, the noise faded. In the stillness, the rabbit scampered back to the warm rails. But the stars still watched the iron beast—pushing through the night.

As Captain of the *Chisholm*, Kol Kellner ordered another change in course. It had been an unexciting day—thank the Lord. Three weeks ago in Ceylon, they'd taken on thousands of bales of raw rubber in addition to white, sticky latex, pumped into cargo tanks. At Cape Town he picked up supplies. The ship rode low and slow in the water, but she was headed home.

His crew of forty Mariners and twenty-five Naval Armed Guard was glad to be headed stateside, no matter how long it took. But the thirty-five Army officers and Navy technicians wanted the damn-quick direct route.

The Captain ignored them and zig-zagged through open waters, making it harder for subs to follow without surfacing or raising their periscopes. The run across the Indian Ocean had been without mishap.

A thin slice of the sun remained above the horizon, blazing brilliant gold splotches across the waves. The Captain walked the deck enjoying the warm breeze.

"At this speed when do you think we'll make port?" Kol watched the officer brace against the hatch. The Army khakis loved riding the waves like peacocks loved swimming pools.

And then both men were floating in air, their arms flailing. The torpedo had hit the third hatch, directly below them. Kol fell to the deck, dazed. He stumbled to his feet, weaving, crashing into railing, willing his legs to get under him.

Above him a Naval Armed Guard wheeled his turret into position, scanning for the sub. One of the Mariners shoved ammunition magazines into the gun.

A white-hot flash shot into the air. A second torpedo hit the hatch by the fo'cas'l. Flames roared along the side of the ship.

By the time the Captain staggered to the conn, the ship listed sharply to starboard. The deck guns became useless, angled at sky or the ocean below them. The Captain looked at his watch: 7p.m. Twilight had come and gone in the excitement. He prayed that the cover of night would save his men. He made the call, "Abandon ship."

Sailors picked up those thrown overboard as they rowed life rafts away. A full moon glinted across the tops of the waves, the reflection of flames, turning the water orange.

The sound of an engine bounced toward them, coming on fast. The sub glided into the nest of lifeboats.

"You will get aboard." The Japanese soldier ordered in perfect English. Behind him, an arsenal of machine guns and pistols pointed at the men. "If you resist, we will shoot all of you."

"I'm Captain Kellner. I want to speak to whoever is in charge." He boarded the sub. From behind, someone walloped his head with a steel pipe. When he came to, his men were being stripped of their life jackets, shirts, I.D. tags, and shoes as they boarded the sub. Their hands were tied behind their backs. An Oiler refused to give up his watch. A Japanese soldier shot him in the head and kicked his body over the side before the Oiler's knees had buckled.

Kol struggled to his feet and received a rifle butt in the small of his back.

The sub's engines started then cruised the waves, looking for more survivors. Shells continued to drop on the *Chisholm* which was still afloat. "Keep your heads down," soldiers screamed at the prisoners who sat half-naked on the fore deck. Men who chanced a peek at their dying ship were beaten with the pipe and slashed with bayonets. Other soldiers dragged men behind the tower. Screams, laughter, and an occasional gun shot rang through the night. None of the Americans came back. Kol sat in front of his men, watching their blood and vomit run between his feet.

A sharp siren pealed. Soldiers ran. "They're diving," Kol yelled, struggling to get to his feet. Moments later, a wall of water poured over the deck, washing men overboard, their hands still tied behind them.

The rush of water momentarily pinned Kol against the conning tower. He pushed himself to the side and swam. It seemed the surface would never come. The moon had set, making the water inky black. The stars watched without concern. In the

168

distance, the *Chishom* burned. Flipping to his back, he floated, trying to keep from rolling side to side.

Another man popped up beside him. "You untied?"

"No. How many made it?"

"I was able to get loose and free five." Someone screamed to their left.

"Sharks," his rescuer said as he untied Kol.

The waves pushed against them as they swam toward the ship. It was all they had in the blackness. Screams crossed the water all night. With the first streaks of dawn, the *Chisholm's* bow tipped down. The propeller upended. It slowly disappeared into the ocean.

They were alone.

A swell lifted Kol. He saw one of the life rafts the Japanese hadn't destroyed, bobbing in a trough of the waves. When he reached it, he could barely pull himself over the side. He lay exhausted and panting. A distant scream drove him into action. He found four more survivors.

There was water and food in the raft. They baked under the tropical sun. At twilight, they heard a familiar whoosh of water.

"No one came to pick you up?" The voice called out in perfect English. From the deck of the sub, soldiers trained machine guns on them. "We've been waiting for your friends, but you cannot count on Americans to rescue their men. Welcome back aboard."

Kol looked into the water. Sharks? Or the Sub?

Aunt Ula sat up. Her nightgown stuck to her sweaty body. She held her head with both hands, willing herself to breathe regularly. This is what happened when stagnant memories were stirred. She hadn't had that dream in years. Some of the events she'd looked up. Some of it was common knowledge after the war. Her right brain tried to help by creatively filling in gaps.

This was bound to happen. She couldn't dig up graves without being haunted by their ghosts, but wasn't this the way to exorcise them? To speak their names aloud and boldly? To expose their stories to the light of day?

Her arms hugged her body. The train rocked her. The wheels hummed their lullaby, slowing the rapid beat of her heart.

"How'd you sleep?" Matty asked when Aunt Ula arrived at their seats the next morning.

"Like I was lying on a bed of nails while wolves circled the room." Aunt Ula gave her an *ignore-me* wave. "In other words, like normal."

"I've already had breakfast, so go ahead. We can talk after."

The old woman squinted one eye. She doubted very much if Matty had eaten. She was still wearing the same dress. Her tape-toed "Bang" boots still lay under the seat.

"Yeah, okay. I'll be back." She returned from the snack car carrying four plates of doughnuts and two chocolate milks. Matty unhinged the fold-down trays. "I'm gonna pray before I eat. Join me." Aunt Ula slapped her hands together.

Matty put her hands in her lap and looked down. She waited. Nothing happened. Keeping her head bowed, she peeked across from her.

Aunt Ula stared. "Pray for yourself. I'm not doing all the work." She closed her eyes.

Matty watched her for moment, studying the wrinkled hands that had built planes, cooked, and God only knew what else. Hands like Nana's. She hoped someone besides her mother was looking out for her grandmother. Please look out for Nana.

"A...men," Aunt Ula announced. "Did you pray or just look at me?"

"I think I prayed. I don't know."

"God's a real good translator of half-garbled prayers. Let's eat. And don't give me that bull about having had breakfast. Haven't you been listening to my story? I know what hungry looks like."

"I'll eat if you'll call your friends. I said I'd be responsible for you and that means checking in."

"Oh...piddle." Aunt Ula shook her chocolate milk.

Matty held out her hand. "Give me the phone. I'll turn it on and queue the number." She asked for names, pushed buttons, and handed the cell back. "It's ringing."

"Hello? Who am I speaking to?" Aunt Ula said.

"You know very well who you've called. Where are you?"

Aunt Ula covered the phone. "It's Vera. A dead person has a better sense of humor than she does." She took a big bite and mumbled around a wad of donut, "Hey, Vera. I'm having about fifteen sugary rolls for breakfast. What're you having?"

"A decent breakfast. Where are you?"

"Lemme talk to Kay. I'll tell *her*." There were fumbling sounds during which Aunt Ula enjoyed shouting into the phone. "I'm losing you. I'm losing you."

"I can hear you just fine. Where are you?"

"Are you about ready to kill that little dog Kitty keeps in her purse? He pees in there you know." More fumbling sounded over the phone. Aunt Ula turned to Matty. "Kitty. Biggest bazoombas you've ever seen." She imitated big melons.

"Why do you say things like that?" Kay's voice came from the phone.

"Because I don't have to ride in a cramped car with a dog that has a bladder the size of a booger. And you'll learn not to put me on speaker."

"Where are you?"

"I transferred to the wrong train, but we figured that out at Billings. We're fixed now. We just went through Sioux Falls. I think I'm heading to Mexico."

Matty stuck out her hand.

"Oh here's that English woman, I'm traveling with. She wants to chat you up." Aunt Ula lowered her voice, "Remember you're British."

Matty rolled her eyes. "Good *mahning*. Our train will be arriving in San Diego near noon. When will you be there?"

"Hello. Well...it depends how many more times we have to stop. Probably not until this evening. You don't sound very English today."

" 'Twas a long night. I'd be happy to make sure Eulalia gets to her hotel, if you'll tell me where you're staying." She listened a moment then said, "Yes, I know where that's—"

Aunt Ula grabbed the phone, telling Kay, "You should really think about taking the train back. Dogs ride in baggage. Okay. I gotta hang up to save the batteries. I intend to go over to Tijuana this afternoon." She ended the call, a smile on her face.

"Why do mess with them?"

"Besides being fun? Control, I think. All they see is an old, wrinkled nut bag. They don't know I had a life before they were born."

"Why don't you tell them?"

"Does anyone listen to old people? Did you when you were in Texas?" Aunt Ula waited for an answer. When one didn't come, she continued. "I live with Vera, who treats me like a child. It's not her fault. She never heard any stories about me as she grew up. My father forbade friends and relatives to speak of me. I was a sinful blotch on the family name—which you'd think would ensure my scandalous reputation getting passed on, but it didn't. Vera only knows this scatty, old woman before you. She's never heard of the young one. I lost my past."

Matty took a donut and shook her chocolate milk carton. "If you'll help me, I'll try to be one of the people who really listen. Do you want to tell me the rest of the story?"

Letters and Laughter

T he reflection in the mirror was different than the one Ula had seen for the last seventeen years. In the past months, she'd grown taller, her face leaner, her eyes deeper with the knowledge of sadness.

Wisdom sketched its marks on the eighteen-year-old face that stared back.

Ula applied red lipstick to lips that were thinner and laughed less often. She studied herself. It wasn't the makeup that made her look different or the hairstyle—longer, falling in careless brown curls to her shoulders.

She knew the exact moment it had begun. It was before she'd enrolled in morning classes to finish her high school degree. It preceded strong-arming Mrs. Bell to become a nurse volunteer. Before she went back to church.

It had been four...no...six months since insight had stuck like lightning, punching the air from her gut and making her slide down the brick wall. She'd sat in the rain on a wet sidewalk. The world had gone in and out of focus. A seaman in his Crackerjack uniform had stopped, fussed, and tried to get her up. She'd pushed him away. She pushed all the helping hands away so she could see her shoe.

The people around her seemed unaffected, unable to hear the truth ringing in her ears. Being adult wasn't about having the right clothes. Or her war efforts to save her brother. As a matter of fact—nothing was about her. That was the simple truth. The whole world could turn just fine without her.

It was about the tiniest ways to help each other through the turning.

For her, wisdom had struck between droplets of rain. A still, small voice whispering while she stared at her shoe on the sidewalk, lying in a puddle.

She'd tossed the other shoe beside it and walked away. Her bare feet registered the cold roughness of the curb, and then stumbled on the uneven concrete where the roots of shade trees had pushed up corners of sidewalk. In front of Mrs. Bell's house, her toes curled into weedy grass. This was how a soul needed to travel—in the grittiness of earth, not on platforms above it. It was the most grounded she'd felt since leaving Oklahoma.

It had taken a while for her roommates to forgive her. An icy chill grew between them. It might have gone on longer if not for Lindell.

No one was particularly looking forward to their group meal, but Ula discovered there was no way to fry their salmon croquettes. The skillets were missing. With anger circling the household like flies, Lindell had the unfortunate timing to walk into the kitchen spouting, "What's knittin', kittens?"

Ula nabbed the little hooligan by the ear and kept hold until he whined a confession. "But I got a free movie ticket for each skillet." The five women marched him down to the local park and made him climb into the chicken wire corral. Over the top of the fence, he handed them fenders, broken bicycles, and old yard tools until he found the skillets.

"Sorry, but we need to cook," Ula apologized to the scowling organizers. In a moment of guilt, she signed Lindell up to become a Scout. "And we'll help run the scrap drives." So each Wednesday morning, the women sat at the park. The forced togetherness made them work out their problems—between accepting cans of grease, bundles of paper, metal bed frames, and gossip.

Mina, through her military connections, found an APO address that was a long shot, but might reach Kol. "It's better than nothing." Ula wrote to him. She asked Lindell to write too. She started over, forging friendships based on truth this time. Wisdom etched another beauty line into her image.

She finished putting on her lipstick and dabbed at the shine on her nose. Big Mae shoulder-bumped her out of the way. "I'm tired of funerals for people I don't know. Since you roped Mrs. Bell into organizing these ceremonies at your church, I've attended more rituals than an undertaker."

Ula side-butted Big Mae from the mirror and finished powdering her face. "She's very good at helping people heal. She understands grief. We only go if there's hardly any family. Think how you'd feel if you gave a son to the war and no one showed up. It's a comfort knowing someone else recognizes the sacrifice."

"But that's just it. There are no bodies. It's not really like a funeral. Death is such a common event anymore. Every day I read the list in the paper. At first, four years ago, I was beside myself when I recognized a name among the missing or dead. But there's been so many since then. It's become common."

"Not to Mrs. Bell. Not to—" A floorboard creaked outside their room. The ladies stopped talking. Lindell peeked around the doorframe.

"Oh, get in here, T.T." Big Mae beckoned to the eleven-year-old. The T.T. stood for Turkey Turd, but since soaping the boy's mouth a few weeks ago, three of the roommates felt they'd better clean up the language they used around him.

Big Mae ferociously dissented, claiming every boy needed to learn to swear. There was an art to it. And she, working at the shipyards with master cussers, was the best person to teach the young man. She'd finally consented to shortening her profanity to initials. "Just as long as everyone knows what they stand for."

"Stop sneaking around. We thought you were Meeny. C'mere." The boy walked dutifully into the room. Big Mae grabbed him by the shoulders, giving him a turn and pushing him down in a chair so she could plaster his cowlick to his skull. "Has the postwoman come?"

"Yeah."

"Was there a letter for Meeny from George?"

Lindell shook his head. "He's dead, isn't he?"

"Shut up." She gave his unruly cowlick a hard smack. "Ula hasn't heard anything either, and she hasn't lost hope." She cast a side-long glance at her roommate. "It takes months to get things sorted out, and even then they don't always get it right. Thankfully, the Dead and Missing Lists are getting smaller each day." She wiped her hands on a towel then pulled on beige gloves as she walked toward the door. "It won't last much longer if we stick together and do our bit." She pointed a gloved finger and stern look at Ula. "But that doesn't mean you're getting me roped into your church."

"Yes..." Ula followed her, "because 'roping' people really makes them want to attend."

"I don't mind going to church." Lindell bounced off the chair. "That's about the only way to get cakes and sweets anymore."

"The car's leaving for Chula Vista in ten minutes," Big Mae yelled. For the past month, on their half-days off, Big Mae had borrowed a neighbor's car for her "picnic and vegetable foray." Buying from the local farmers didn't take any blue ration stamps, which she traded for meat coupons. Any extra produce the women didn't use, she sold or traded for gas.

Ula sat by a window on these outings. The land with miles of fields, short trees, and few people reminded her of home. Mina chose a window seat too. The farms gave her the hope of growing things. Her late winter Victory garden wasn't yielding much, and seeds were getting hard to come by. She'd tried drying them on newspapers in Mrs. Bell's garage, but Lindell had found the yellowed papers and traded them for a movie ticket in the paper drive.

Mina clutched her pocket as the countryside flew by the window. As usual, she'd waited on the front porch for the mail. Just before they'd left, the postwoman arrived. With a smile, she'd put the letter in Mina's hand before pushing the rest of the mail through the door slot. It was in George's handwriting. He was alive. That was enough. She'd stuffed it in her pocket. She'd find a quiet place to read it. Just her and George.

Big Mae passed their customary stand. A weathered board across the door, lettered in barn paint, read *Closed*. "Every week, there are fewer markets and more *For Sale* signs on the fences." They ended up in the small farming-community of Montgomery, parking the old DeSoto next to a lean-to with bushels of squash and carrots in front. Big Mae pulled two empty baskets out from the trunk and gave a single clap. "I'm horse-trading. The rest of you scout out a spot for our picnic."

Mina, toting a water jug, walked barren, humped rows of what used to be a celery field toward the only tree around. Ula followed, lugging the picnic box. Peg and Lindell scanned the skies, trying out the plane spotter card that had come bundled in his chewing gum.

"Look at this poor dirt." Dust puffed with each of Ula's steps.

"The big companies sucked the life out of it after the Jap farmers made it arable." Mina called over her shoulder as she walked. "Now that there's noise about the war ending, they're abandoning this dustbowl."

Ula lumbered to catch up. "I remember Mama making Joe and me cover our faces with wet bandanas when the black blizzards rolled through Oklahoma." She kicked the dirt. "This isn't that bad. It still has some topsoil, but they need to do something soon or it'll be in the wind."

Mina watched Ula spread an old army blanket under a small, misshapen locust tree. "Look at this." Kneeling, Ula pulled up tiny saplings which had sprouted in the fence line. "Too bad no one cares enough to take care of this place."

"I left something. Go ahead and start." Mina called as she ran back to the car.

Ula gave her a quizzical look, but the other women had arrived with chatter and more food. When all was set out, Peg pulled the lid off of Ula's old lard-can lunch pail. She took out a piece of fried chicken and passed the can along. "Well, as usual, I had to referee."

Big Mae made a face. "There's an art to dickering—"

"Oh, not everything has to be a baker's dozen, you know." Peg threw a napkin at her.

"What's that sound?" Lindell held a boiled egg and a chicken leg, as he cocked his ear toward the sky.

A low keening came from the Desoto.

"Meeny?"

Lindell was first to arrive, even though he was weighted with the can of fried chicken under his arm. He stared at Mina, sitting in the open door of the back seat, her feet on the ground, her arms clutching herself as she rocked and moaned.

"Mama!" He grabbed, his mother when she ran up.

"Meeny. What is it?" Big Mae took her by the shoulders.

"I can't do this anymore. I can't." Mina's face contorted, her eyes becoming watery slits.

Ula squeezed next to Big Mae. Very softly, she whispered, "Cry, Mina. Cry. He was a good man."

"No." Mina unwrapped her arms from her body. "He sent a letter." A V-mail lay crushed in her hand. "He's alive."

Big Mae leaned back, knocking Ula out of the way as she flung her arms wide. "You're bawling because he's alive? Damn. What a relief. Wait. The jackass isn't ditching you, is he?"

"No." Mina wailed, shaking the letter. "He's been reassigned as a belly gunner."

The women stared.

"Mama? Isn't that good? He's alive. He'll sit here, won't he?" Lindell pointed to the Plexiglass bubble at the bottom of the B-17 on his spotter card.

Mrs. Bell pulled Lindell away from the group, her arm around his shoulders as he hung onto her waist. "You mustn't ask her anything about it," she whispered. "Promise me, Lindell. Not a word."

"Why?"

"Because that bubble is the first thing the *Luftwaffe* shoot in every battle."

"Play catch the bottle, Li'l Okie—please?" The voice traveled up the ladder into the tail of the ship. Ula sat on her tool box, teaching the new girl how to install ejector chutes for used ammunition.

"Go help him, Iowa." Ula gave a sideways nod toward the exit. "I'll finish this." The young woman had the look of a frightened rabbit that Ula knew so well. "Just stand at the top, Gladys, and catch the oxygen bottles he tosses from below. If he can't find a sucker to help him, he has to climb up and down the ladder about twenty times."

Ula finished and began hanging the green-yellow bottles in loop-straps. "Hey," she yelled down the ladder, "Remember, you owe Iowa one for helping you."

"He grinned as he tossed a bottle. "You know I always take care of—"

A short whistle blast squealed over his words. Workers looked at their watches, confused. Life at the plant was ordered by the whistle: lunch time, smoke time, quitting time. This one had no meaning.

"Attention. Attention, please," a male voice boomed over the plant's loud speakers.

Drills, motors, and cranes stopped. People came out of ships, prepared to run from an attack or dance because the war had ended.

"President Franklin D. Roosevelt had a massive stroke and died this evening. While we grieve for the passing of our beloved president, it will not slow our efforts. President Harry Truman has vowed to finish President Roosevelt's march to victory. We will now observe a moment of silence. May he rest in God's peace."

For the first time, in years, the huge room that birthed weapons went totally quiet. It wasn't the sacred silence Ula experienced at the convent, but a waiting stillness like the moment before an exam is turned over and the answers can be filled in.

At the end of two minutes the short whistle blew. The plant roared back into life.

When Ula arrived home, at 2:30 that morning, the others were in the kitchen. Lindell hid behind the chair in the living room. "Go to bed," she said as she passed him. The women drank hot tea or Sanka, discussing the President and war gossip.

"This came for you." Mrs. Bell handed her an envelope. Flourishes of her mother's penmanship curled around her name. She read the short note, lay it on the table, and went outside to sit on the porch.

Peeper frogs sang high and low notes, filling the damp air with their chorale. The smell of wet dirt promised an end to barren trees and chilly nights. A few bright stars winked in the sky. The door creaked. Footsteps padded across the porch. A small person in pajamas sat next to her. "Where do you think they go when they die?" Lindell asked, looking at the stars.

"Heaven, hon." Ula followed his gaze.

"Do they watch us?"

"I don't...know." Her words faded as though there was no air to push them out.

Lindell slipped his arm around her and leaned his head against her side. "Do you think your brother will meet my dad in heaven?"

"I do." She sniffed.

"And the President?"

She nodded. "I bet they're sitting on a star with God right now, telling stories and chuckling."

"That's a lot of laughter. 'Cause there's lots more stars than this. I saw 'em all once, out in the country."

"They're happy. They're all finally at peace."

"I wish I was happy too."

"We will be again. I promise." Ula slipped her arm around him. "Someday we'll smile when we look at the stars. Just not for a while."

The roommates watched from the dark living room, silent, the letter in Mrs. Bell's hand.

Ula and the boy sat on the top porch step, watching the heavenly lights inch across the sky. They let their thoughts fade into the night and the peeping of the frogs. Each waited and hoped—if they were still enough, if they listened hard enough— they'd hear faint laughter from the stars.

Lipstick Address

*I*n the following weeks, Ula's brain stayed in a fog. She had long suspected Joe was dead. To see it in writing made her numb. She barely slept. There were no dreams. She'd always thought if her brother left this earth, he'd drop by in that moment between her wakefulness and sleep to say good bye. He hadn't. He was gone. Simply gone.

Mr. Dillard teamed her with Delbert to do pipe installations. The lanky fellow was slow and always behind, but he was thorough. He'd watch out for her, make sure everything was tightened and keep her from stepping backwards off a ladder because she was in a daze.

To Ula, it felt like punishment. The ships had hundreds of yards of metal tubing. Much of it pre-formed to go around windows, belt frames, and switchboxes. It rarely fit correctly. Many pieces had to be re-bent or customized. The tiniest tubes, called pipes, carried a de-icing agent from the fore to the aft. She hated it most of all. Of course, that's mostly what she handled because her small body could crawl into the rabbit holes on the ship.

As the whistle blew, ending the 11 p.m. break, she walked down the center aisle surveying the ships. They entered the building in three pieces, and were joined together to make a fuselage. Moving up the line, they sprouted wings and guts. As they rounded the horseshoe turn, they shone with Plexiglass nose cones and revolving turrets, by the end, they were stuffed with wires, hoses, radios, giant propellers and more guns. They would be towed out the door and flown to a field where air crewmen would paint names on their sides like: Dinah Might, Iza Vailable, Any Time Annie, or Miss Conduct. Then they would fly through bullets and anti-air craft shells, until they had so many wounds they would fall back to the ground—in Turkey or Tokyo, or far from where they were born. It made her sad for both the planes and the men.

"Hey!" Delbert grabbed her arm, jerking her thoughts sideways. "Good news! The small pipes we've been missing for two days just came in. Damn Red Buttons are screaming for us to catch up. ASAP."

"Whoopie," Ula said.

"You told me you've always wanted to go in the field. We only need one toolbox. I'll put mine in my locker and get an armload of pipes. Meet you by the door."

Delbert was right. She'd always wanted to go outside and inspect the finished result of her labors. Why wasn't she more excited now that it was really happening? For weeks it had been hard to make decisions. Even the choice between an apple or extra carrots for lunch was bewildering.

A hooded light hung over the plant's back door. Somewhere in the blackness in front of her were a dozen planes, waiting like resting whales because they were missing a small section of pipe.

"Ake uh ight." Delbert appeared next to her, his arms full of aluminum tubes, his mouth full of flashlight. Ula took it and turned it on. "We start at the front." He led the way to the farthest plane. "Our goal is to work backwards down the line 'til we're at our own station."

"We'll never make that tonight." Ula checked her watch.

"But, we'll get the field done, so the girls can take these ships tonight."

Inside the first bomber, Delbert lifted a section of the washboard flooring, opening the entrance to a small cavity. Ula pulled her big wrench from her back pocket, putting it on the floor next to the hole. She lay on her back, holding the flashlight, and squirmed inside the tiny space until only her feet showed.

"Why do you carry this one-inch box end all the time?" His hand grazed the wrench as he picked up a pipe. "You workin' on engines, now?" He stuck the tubing and small tools she needed into the hole.

Her hand appeared and grabbed them. "Gator repellant." Her voice carried a smile. "I wave it like a wand, and he goes somewhere else."

"You shouldn't have to put up with that. You oughta become one of those Women Air Force Service Pilots. You've got the smarts to fly these planes outta here. They'd train you."

"I'm not that gutsy. Those gals tow targets for artillery practice too. If they crash, the family has to get the body home. The government doesn't help since they're not military. No Thanks." Ula rapped on metal, signaling she wanted another pipe.

"Same as you or me." He stuck another piece into the opening. "If I'd cracked your skull when I dropped that wrench your first day, your family woulda had to haul you to Oklahoma."

"Then I'd probably be buried here. Out back of this building."

"Nobody'd come get you?"

A long moment passed before Ula muttered, "Not anymore."

When she was done, he grabbed her by the feet and pulled her out. She picked up her weapon-wrench from the floor and stuck it back in her pocket.

"Don't go packin' up," Delbert reminded her as he pulled a tag from the floor and ripped it in half: *Parts to be installed here.* "Now we do this eleven more times."

It was the last plane and ten minutes before quitting when they ran low on tubes. "I'll pull you out and we'll call it good," Delbert said into the hole.

"No." Ula groaned. "Let's get this over with. Hand me what you've got and run for more pipes. And Delbert? Run. It's creepy in here."

She finished as much as she could and turned off the light. It was quiet. Too quiet. She could squirm out, but she doubted if she could make herself get back in when Delbert came. Slapping the sides of her shoes together, she hummed a tune to take the edge off the nothingness.

She didn't hear his footsteps. It was the sound of sliding metal that made her jump. "Delbert?" With a *bang*, the washboard section of flooring dropped over the hole. "Delbert!" she yelled louder. "This isn't funny." She bucked and jerked her feet, raising the flooring slightly. A clanging *thud* told her the toolbox had been set on top of her chamber. The flooring wouldn't move.

The plane was quiet. Both people listened to the other. Then a slight scraping of metal to the right of the cavity let her know someone had picked up her box end wrench. Very quietly, like a high, happy note, a voice said, "Whoops!" Footsteps walked away.

Ula screamed. It hurt her ears in the tiny space. She kicked, but with only a few inches above her toes, there wasn't enough leverage to move the flooring.

Delbert would be back. Then she'd find that jackboot thug and teach him a lesson—using a bigger wrench. She sang to calm herself, "I'll be seeing you..." Delbert would bring more pipe. Soon. Probably by the time she reached the second stanza.

Her watch showed twenty minutes had passed. She flicked the flashlight off. Earlier, when she'd noticed the bulb dimming, it had sent her into a panic. Now she kept it off until the confinement and blackness made her screech and beat on the metal in a frenzied fit. This must have been what Tommy felt. Trapped in a hole. No way to leave.

But death wasn't dropping out of the sky. Safety was nearby. She felt a bit silly for being so dramatic. This was a prank. Spiteful payback. All she had to do was stay alert and listen for the WASP to arrive. And what if they didn't hear her before firing up the plane? She'd end up at an air force base across the country. That's all. If she didn't freeze en route. If the fly girls even came tonight.

To calm herself, she began scratching her name on the metal. It was forbidden, but G.I.s left "Kilroy was here" all over Europe. Why not? What else did she have to do? When her fingers got tired, she wormed her hand into her pocket, pulled out her lipstick and finished the job. She stared at her name in Helena Rubenstein's *Apple Red* on the flooring above her. She added her address. For some reason, it felt good. In case something happened, she'd left her mark. She'd been here. She'd done something. Her legacy.

She sighed. Her father must be so proud to have a son who'd dodged all but one bullet and a daughter who made machines that killed someone's brother or son.

Letting out a big breath, she closed her eyes and turned off the flashlight. "I'm sorry, Lord. Sorry I have to be held down before I'll stop long enough to talk with you..."

"I'd know those shoes anywhere!" The woman's voice was excited.

Someone grabbed Ula's feet and pulled her from the hole. She squinted, holding up a hand to block the light shining in her eyes.

"That idiotic bastard. I'll have his head!" Mr. Dillard shouted. "Are you okay, Li'l Okie? He'll lose his defense deferment so fast, he'll be peeking out of a foxhole by the end of this week."

"Were you asleep?" The woman asked.

The foreman grabbed Ula's hand. "Your knuckles are bleeding." He began wrapping it, mumbling curses.

Ula could see they were having their moment of indignation and shock, but she'd already had hers an hour ago and moved on. "I'm okay." Closing one eye and squinting the other, she pushed the light out of her face. "It wasn't Delbert."

They walked back to the plant. Mr. Dillard's arm was around Ula so tightly, few of her footsteps actually touched the ground. The woman followed them to an office, lugging the tool box.

As soon as they were through the door, the foreman called off the armed military personnel, searching the plant.

The woman set the toolbox down heavily. Ula recognized her as the time keeper who checked on her throughout the shift. "I can't leave until all the time cards are punched out and accounted for. And Mr. Dillard can't leave until I leave." She jumped as the foreman slammed the phone down behind her.

"Delbert's just been brought in. I sent personnel to haul his ass back here." His nostrils were white-rimmed. "I'm sorry I didn't find you earlier, Li'l Okie. I looked in the field, but the planes were closed. I figured you were somewhere else in the plant. He was supposed to watch out for you—"

"It was Gator." Ula cut into his tirade. "Delbert went to get more pipes so we could finish up. While I was in the hole, Gator put the flooring down."

"You know this how?"

"He took my box end wrench, which I take out of my pocket and slap against my palm whenever he comes around, and he made a little *oops* noise."

"Mr. Gaither was by the gates when the search started." Lines of fury creased the foreman's forehead. "He said he hadn't seen either of you all evening."

188

"That's bullshit." Delbert shouted as two soldiers pushed him into the room. "I was on my way back to Ula when Gator told me she'd already packed up and left. I looked outside. The planes were buttoned up tight I would never—"

"I know you wouldn't." Ula gave the skinny man a tired smile.

"Well, somebody's lying." Mr. Dillard said.

Delbert glanced up at the guards on either side of him. "Then why don't you haul him back in here too?"

"It doesn't matter." Ula yawned. "It really doesn't matter."

"Did you fall asleep out there?" The timekeeper asked.

Ula smiled sadly as she stood. "I know you have to get to the bottom of this, Mr. Dillard, but for me...it actually worked out for the best. I've been in a fog lately, and now I know exactly what I need to do. But for now..." she looked at the timekeeper. "I'd like to clock out and go home."

This time it was a proper "leaving." At the end of the following week, Ula gave notice. She said a suitable goodbye to the folks at Station 18. Mr. Dillard gave her a hug. "Sorry. We couldn't prove Mr. Gaither did it, but he'll be transferred when he gets better." He stopped her question with a head shake and a concerned look that wasn't convincing. "Somebody used him as a punching bag last night as he was on his way home. Nobody seems to have seen a thing. I guess there's a lot of that going around." He patted her shoulder. "Remember, Ula. You built bombers. You can do anything."

As she and Mina stood near the gates, Bab, leader of The Reds, passed her. "Here kid. I hope you don't need this wherever you're going." She stuffed her green hair turban into Ula's pocket and walked on.

"I've seen everything now." Mina's eyes were big. "This calls for a celebration."

"I'll buy the first round." Delbert and several fellows from Station 18 surrounded them. "We got this for you." He pushed a sack into Ula's hands. Even through the paper, she knew the feel of it. "Thanks." Ula nodded.

They walked past Gate Two, and she set her toolbox down. "Tell the others I'll catch up. I need a second." Pulling her box end wrench from the sack, she smacked it against her palm as she turned and looked back. Camouflage covered the area with the secret feeling of being under a blanket. In the darkness, large buildings were invisible except for their bright lights, shining through half-opened doors. Ant-sized figures climbed, bent, stooped, and knelt. Already, that part of her life was starting to push away and feel distant. She stuck her wrench in her tool box, locked the lid, and carried it to the bus one last time.

She wrote the nuns. She wrote her mother. She wrote Kol.

"I'm going back to the farm," she told her roommates. "But not the farm in Oklahoma. I bought a little place near Chula Vista."

"You're not old enough to own land," Big Mae said.

"I didn't think so either, so I had help, but the banker seemed very anxious to get the loan off his books. Smith Produce got it when they auctioned off the Japanese farms. They only made payments for two years. It's been in arrears for a while. Kol left me money. This is what I want to spend it on. Nobody asked my age. I think they were glad to have a paying customer."

"Oh, honey." Peg shook her head. "I hate to tell you this, but if it sounds too good to be true, it's probably a scam. You may not see that money again."

"Mina?" Ula turned to her housemate. "Did it seem on the up and up to you?"

"You were in on this?" Peg's voice took on an accusatory tone.

"I'm sick of war all around me. Sick of building airplanes and waiting for a telegram. I want to make something that doesn't kill people. I put George's and my savings in the property, too. This war won't last forever."

Everyone started talking at once, except Mrs. Bell who nearly fainted with the thought of losing two renters.

In the first month, Ula dragged herself from the field each evening, groaning, "Why did we do this?"

"I don't know." Mina laid her head on the kitchen table. "I thought I'd get to wear dresses again." She stuck out her muck-covered foot. "Now I wear leaky boots and coveralls. The good news is, we're not required to wear head coverings." But they did.

The next four months were more grueling than they'd imagined. There were no whistles for quitting time. No half-days off. From dawn to dusk, they worked in the fields. They'd been able to clean only one bedroom in the dilapidated farmhouse, but they rarely used it, often falling asleep in their dirty clothes on a threadbare couch or the back porch immediately after taking off their boots. Families of mice lived in the rooms. Only half of the kitchen was useable, and Ula swore she'd seen a box turtle crawling under the stove.

"Well, he'll have to stay there till summer harvest is over." Mina sat at the shaky, chrome-legged kitchen table, planning a planting chart. Whenever she had energy, she'd calculate crop yield and seed costs until Ula would turn out the lights, saying, "Go to bed; you're keeping the turtle up."

They brought in ladies from the Women's Land Army, who helped with spring planting. Ula figured life must be tough in

Los Angeles if these city women volunteered to live in railway box cars and grow calluses for seventy cents an hour.

"War requires food." Mina shrugged. "Besides, if you figure *our* hours and pay, we make less than they do."

Ula bought third-hand equipment, a 1939 Chevy truck and a '32 Oliver tractor. Their one farm hand, Lane, kept the machines jury-rigged together and running. Both Ula and Mina couldn't stomach him, but they needed his skills. He was thirty, too good-looking, and claimed to have a bad hip and a good agricultural deferment so he could stay out of the war. The bad hip didn't keep him from dancing on Saturday nights, but it did require a lot of rest the following Sunday morning.

Their "C" ration card for agriculture allowed them extra gasoline. Lane cussed each jaunt to the local dairy farmer to help sling oozing manure into the truck bed. He saved his special vocabulary for San Diego's packing plants, mumbling "sonufabitchin' fish" each time they wrestled with a barrel of guts. He did whatever he could to get out of taking his turn on the tractor. Ula thought the monotony of plowing up and down the fields, working fish heads or cow dung into the soil was relaxing. Lane kept up a constant rant, "Damn stink smells all the way to the next county."

With the WLA's help, they harvested a spring crop and made a summer planting. Under a mid-August sun, Ula worked with the land girls, hoeing carrots. In the next field, a small dust cloud followed Mina chugging back and forth on the tractor, turning the fish dirt again so it would be ready for fall.

A flatbed truck came down the road in front of the property, driving sixty to nothing, honking. The driver hung half-way out the window, his passenger doing the same as they beat on the doors, whooping and hollering.

The ladies laughed, watched them pass then went back to hoeing. "Country life is great," Ula said. "There's enough room to test the home brew before it's capped and not kill anyone in the process."

A loud *boom* sounded from the little town a few miles away. Ula saw nothing, no smoke nor flames. The land girls looked at each other. Mina hadn't heard it and continued aggravating the dirt with her tractor.

Lane ran out of the extra sleeping quarters, which he called the bunkhouse, waving his arms and hollering. He got to Mina first. She stopped the tractor, got off to talk, and then began screaming.

Ula strained to hear their words, but the wind shifted, carrying them to the south.

She saw Mina hug Lane. There was only one reason she would do that.

The war was over.

More cars were coming down the road, flashing their lights, honking, people yelling. Lane ran to the end of the drive and hopped on the back of a truck heading toward town.

Mina who had never once uttered a word about God had fallen to her knees in the dirt and appeared to be crying and praying. The land girls were hugging each other.

Ula dropped her hoe and walked away. She stopped at the small rise above the house, the highest spot in her flat world. She'd planted a puny peach tree there. A misshapen little thing she'd been given because it was dying. No matter how tired she was, each night she'd carried a bucket of water to the sapling, given it a drink, then had sat on the bucket, surveying her empire.

Now she turned in a slow circle. The WLA ladies were headed to the house. The sound of fireworks drifted from town. A beautiful, late summer day. Birds dipped and flew from tree to tree, unconcerned about the honking trucks. The sun inched at the same speed it always had toward the horizon. Fall crops would soon be planted. Tomorrow they'd move the steers to another pasture. The world would go on as usual. One day they were at war, and one day they weren't. And in between? How many lives had been uprooted? Families torn apart? People on both sides dead, their graves not even known?

Ula looked at the sky, seeking the face of God—who she knew was listening to both the noise and Mina's prayers. She asked over and over, "What was it all for?"

Peach Hill Farm

*A*unt Ula suddenly stood. "I recognize the old mill. We're in San Diego."

Matty quickly turned, checking her bearings through the window. She couldn't identify the crumbling, red brick building. It was just some decrepit place in the industrial area. She was having trouble surfacing from the depths of World War II. For a moment, it was easy to imagine these structures being new. Their windows unbroken, mortar filling each crack, train cars waiting on side rails, men and women loading supplies to be shipped to troops.

A bum lying in a doorway shot the finger at the train, and the images blinked away, replaced by drifts of debris in corners, rusted downspouts and signs missing from their yard arms.

Aunt Ula was gone. No sign of her up and down the aisle. Matty quickly stuffed everything into her knapsack and slipped on her boots. She grabbed the paper plates from breakfast and tried to keep her shoulder bag from banging heads as she walked down the aisles.

The old lady was standing in the luggage landing, coat on, gripping her extended-handle roll-along-bag. "Where're you going? We've got a few minutes to finish the story."

"I'm afraid not, dear. I've got someplace to be."

"I said I'd take you to your hotel. You can tell me on the way."

"I'm not going to the hotel. I may have to finish up without you, dear."

***

"This is Beater Bug," Matty said as Aunt Ula got in the old VW. "It doesn't look like much, but it got me from Clarksville, Texas to here." First gear growled as she took off and then bucked it into second. "Now where are we going?" Aunt Ula handed her an envelope, bent at the corners. "This is from you to your mother?" Matty scanned the postmark. "1946?" Both eyebrows rose as she looked at the old woman.

"Just go to the return address."

Matty tapped the location into Mapfinder on her cell phone. "I told your friends I'd get you to your hotel. I didn't think that meant a side-trip to the valley, but..." She shrugged.

"I'm looking for something. What're you waiting for?" Aunt Ula pointed to the light which had barely turned from red to green. "We're burning daylight here."

"We'll get there. Relax. The war may have ended, but you've got a lot of loose ends to wrap up. What're you looking for?"

Aunt Ula let out a snort. "You know who knocked on my door two days later? Well, I assume they knocked, I didn't hear them. Nobody uses the front door in the country. I don't think it would even open. Mina and I were in the north field, trying to teach cattle, which are even stupider than turkeys, where the gate was to greener pastures. I looked up, and traipsing across the field, picking their feet up real high so they wouldn't step in cow patties, came Mrs. Bell, Lindell, and my former room-mates.

"Lindell took off, chasing steers. I let him. He couldn't hurt anything, and if he happened to get close enough to get kicked, it might knock some sense into him. The problem was Big Mae." Aunt Ula looked to the heavens and shook her head.

"The end of the war came bingo-bango. Everybody cele-brated. Danced in the streets. The next day Big Mae went to work—the gates were chained shut. The women—just the women—were told they weren't needed anymore. The line stretched eight blocks long. They were locked out. The company would send their paychecks. Big Mae's tools were still in her locker. She was ready to strangle somebody."

"They kicked them out just like that?"

"Seven days a week for five years, then 'goodbye,' 'get out.' Posters went up all over town, encouraging women to step aside so a returning vet would have a job. It was a different time, dear. Most women were glad to get out of slacks and back into dresses. They'd been working full time, raising kids, and taking care of everyone else. They felt it was finally their turn to rest. But my roommates didn't know what they were going to do. So Peach Hill Farm grew from two women and a worthless farmhand to five women, and a boy. We fired Lane. Mrs. Bell put her house up for sale; she couldn't count on renters anymore.

"We all got along surprisingly well. Mrs. Bell cleaned and trapped about a thousand mice—who would've thought she had it in her? Big Mae took to farming—turn here, dear. I recognize this corner."

"That's not what the map lady says." Matty glanced at the screen.

"She's not from here and doesn't have a clue. Turn. Turn. TURN!" Aunt Ula shouted.

Matty hit the brakes. "Don't yell at me." Her voice was thorny. "We're both tired and hungry. I'm stopping somewhere. You need to eat something. You're getting pushy, and I'm getting snotty." She put her hand on the gearshift, but Aunt Ula placed her hand on top of it.

The old woman gave her a nun's stare, her words quiet and serious. "Please don't talk to me that way. Don't treat me like a child. I know I'm anxious and acting like one, but you now know the deepest part of my past. No one is aware of what I once accomplished. Vera, my only relative, tells me where to go, what to eat, and chides me for saying silly things. No one asks for my opinion or what I want to do about myself. It's hard being very young or very old."

Matty stared at the fields. "I'm sorry. I suppose we all think we know better. That an old person has lost touch with...what's best."

Aunt Ula took her hand off Matty's, a sad smile on her lips. "What's important...changes with age."

Matty nodded. "I'm hungry. Would you mind if we stopped and picked up some burgers? I can drive and eat at the same time."

Aunt Ula smiled. "Make sure wherever you stop has ice cream too. There's a town if you had turned back where I told you to."

Matty sighed, backed up and turned. They found a drive-in—not the one Aunt Ula remembered, "...but that was years ago." The old woman slurped her chocolate malted.

"So you all became one big happy family."

"No. We became a company. Peach Hill Produce. Mina's husband, George, came home from the war. He was good at bookkeeping. Peg was great at sales. And Big Mae...she did the mechanical tough stuff and played sheriff. She kept a shotgun by the door. If a chicken squawked or a cow mooed at night, she was out the door, *Blam! Blam!* shooting coyotes or skunks or the air. It gave our war vets heart attacks. They'd jump two feet high and run into the yard in their underwear, brandishing knives, thinking they were under attack."

"Vets? You had more than one? Did Tommy or Kol come home?"

"Tommy didn't make it back. Neither did any of the letters, I sent to him. I like to think some other boy got them. I hope it helped. And Kol...yes, he came home—in a way."

"What d'ya mean?'"

"I told you Mrs. Bell volunteered as a nurse? Sometimes she brought wounded vets home for dinner. Their nerves were shot. The country quietness was good for them. One night she held our door open for one of her patients. He gimped in, bent over, a limp on his right side. I didn't recognize Kol. War ages a man, but prison camp had rotted a big hunk out of his soul. He'd been so handsome, but his hair was thin, his cheeks sucked in like a skeleton, a big scar ran down the side of his face. I thought he'd snap when I hugged him. He only weighed ninety-five pounds." Aunt Ula stared out the window. "And that was after the hospital had fattened him up a bit.

"We sat down to eat, and he siphoned down a whole glass of milk in a few seconds. We didn't mean to stare, but.... Then Mina's husband, George, chugged his milk, asked for more, and ordered a round for Kol too. Next, he requested chopped lettuce. Those guys ate three heads of lettuce that night.

Kol was too proud to ask for help, but I went to see a nurse who worked with POWs coming from the Philippines. Many of the men were so malnourished, they'd gone blind. Kol had regained his sight, but not his spirit. The scars all over his body weren't as deep as the ones in his mind."

"They had help for him didn't they?"

"Very little. The Merchant Marine wasn't military. He couldn't visit Vet Hospitals. He had no benefits. He was paid while afloat, but received only a dollar a day as a POW. He had little money, and I had spent his life savings on a farm. I never expected him to come back, really."

"This seems so wrong."

"He stayed in the bunkhouse, worked like a farmhand. Said he'd never saddle me with the broken shell he'd become. Lindell had the most healing effect on him. Together, they started a turtle farm, of all things. Anytime we came upon a turtle, we'd have to rescue it. They built a fenced area, fed 'em, dug hidey holes. Lindell got Kol to talk, not about the war, but other things. You know kids. He was in awe of the bulbs of flesh on Kol's fingers where they'd pulled his fingernails out several times. He'd been a prisoner for almost a year. Lindell treated Kol like he was cooler than a Slinky toy.

"Every evening, after supper, I'd walk up to Peach Hill. After a while, a bucket would quietly settle beside mine and he'd sit down. We didn't speak. We didn't need to. It was a time of sacred silence again. We'd watch the sky turn purple and pink and the sun slip to another day.

"He got better, stronger. The limp became minor. His fingertips were fleshy, but he could use them. Most of the nails grew back. People told him how lucky he was to have work after the war, a place to stay, and people that cared. He'd agree. It was a lie.

I'd secretly watch him in the fields. He was a hard worker, but there was no joy in it. It was as though he was punishing himself for his Mariners who died. He'd locked himself in a prison camp of land and fields, doing work he hated. His body may have been getting stronger, but his spirit faded. Some people heal by working the soil, but he was drying up, like a starfish too long out of water.

"One day a letter arrived, covered with postmarks, forwarded from Mrs. Bell's old address. I was sitting on my bucket on the hill, reading it, when Kol arrived with manure. He'd nursed, fertilized, and fussed with that little peach tree until it was looking good. The letter said a plane had been hit in the last days of the war. She'd gotten the men home, but the wheels wouldn't drop. The pilot slid in, tearing up the belly of the plane. When they were fixing her, they found my name and address in red lipstick across the underside of a floor panel. He sent a note signed by him and his crew, thanking me for building the plane that saved their lives.

Matty braked Beater Bug, reached over, and turned off the cell phone. "I can't listen with that map-lady talking."

Aunt Ula's eyes were shiny. Her words were barely louder than the wind in the leaves of the orange trees around them. "You know what Kol said?" Matty shook her head.

"Wasn't it time I counted the lives I had saved, making those planes, rather than carrying the weight of my father's damning judgment and the brother I couldn't save? Wasn't it time to let go?

"So I asked him, 'Isn't it time you count the thousands of lives you transported safely, and release the ones you couldn't bring home? I need you, Kol. I waited for you. Faithfully. It will get better.

"He cried. First and only time I ever saw him do that." She let out a breath and tapped the steering wheel. "Better get going."

Matty put the VW through its gears as Aunt Ula continued, "For my nineteenth birthday, he built a stone bench for us on Peach Hill. We put mementos in an ammo box, and he sealed it into the support pillar. I put in my ration book and my box end wrench."

"What did he put in?"

"That's what we're about to find out." Aunt Ula grinned and raised her eyebrows. "It was a secret. The only clue he gave me was, 'Remember how we promised we'd always leave a message if we had to go? Your message is in there.' "

"Holy mooing cow. We're going to unearth a time capsule? Do we need tools?"

"We can get them from the farm."

"You still own it?"

"No. Kol refused to take me away from the company I'd built. So I sold out to George and Mina. Now I had nothing, except Kol's original money and some extra."

"You sacrificed everything for him?"

"It didn't feel like I gave up a thing. We bought a boat and sailed the world, lived on an island for seven years. Kol was smart about supplies and sea trade. I even got to wear beautiful shoes that were bad for my feet again, but that's another story. They were some of the happiest days of my life. Why're we stopping?"

"Because...we're here." Matty looked around, a pained stare on her face.

"This is a drugstore and a..."Aunt Ula leaned forward squinting through the window. "A fancy-pants dress shop."

"This is the address. I turned off the map-lady so she'd quit saying it. I didn't want to upset you. I've been driving in a grid pattern for the last fifteen minutes." Matty's voice notched up a note. "I thought maybe it was around here somewhere, but it's all stores and houses."

They got out of the car. Aunt Ula stared at the sidewalks, fire hydrants, and lampposts lining the street like sentries.

"This can't be right," Matty said. "George and Mina would've told you, wouldn't they?" Aunt Ula wandered the street, her eyes searching for anything familiar. She stared at a sign. Matty joined her, putting her hand under the old woman's arm. "Let's sit down."

The metal, ventilated bench was anchored to the sidewalk next to the sign for Peach Hill Plaza.

"I don't know why I thought it would all be here." Aunt Ula traced her finger over the holes in the bench. "I'm an idiot."

"George and Mina?" Matty urged. "Did they tell you?"

"We exchanged Christmas cards. But even those eventually stopped." Aunt Ula stared. "Big Mae and Lindell died. Her tractor rolled as she went up an embankment. Lindell was riding behind her. It took the stuffing out of George and Mina. They wrote that they'd sold to the Japanese. The land finally went back to the original owners, which seemed right to me. I never thought they'd stop farming though."

"You and Kol never came back to visit?"

"We were overseas. I didn't keep in touch. I let those friendships fade away. When he passed, I didn't have the heart to return—until now."

"Kids?"

"Aunt Ula shook her head. "Kol couldn't...not after the torture."

"I'm so sorry. How long since he...?" Matty shook her head. "Sorry. It doesn't matter."

"I used to be able to tell you to the day. Then it mushed into years. Every Oklahoma storm reminds me how we tried to make harbor, but didn't reach it. A gale came up at night. The mast cracked. He put me in the covered raft. I fought with him about it. I thought we could weather it out. I'd seen him pull us out of squalls that fish didn't even survive through, but he knew. He was always calm at sea. He could read the waves.

"He took my face in both hands, kissed me hard and long, then looked me in the eye and said, 'You've never obeyed me before, so this time...thanks for leaving. Stay in the raft.' That's when I got scared. He pushed the raft off and dropped the tether rope, yelling, 'See you on the other side.'

"I left the zipper open an inch or two so I could see him. Each wave took me farther away. He had on a life vest—which was strange—and stayed at the radio, shouting our location over and over.

"That's the last image I have of him. I never saw the wave that hit us. I think I rolled twice. I don't know. Several more waves swamped me. I could hear myself screaming, and then only the roar of the storm.

"The mast had to have broken, dragging the boat down, taking on water even if it had landed right-side up. It was night, but being entombed in the dark didn't scare me. Being alone did. In an hour, the Puerto Rican Coast Guard picked me up. They would've never found me if Kol hadn't stayed on the radio. They searched but never found a piece of the boat. He was gone."

They sat quietly, the twilight turning to dusk. After a while, Matty shifted on the bench. "You okay?" Aunt Ula nodded without looking at her. The young woman arose. "Maybe someone knows what happened to the time capsule. I'm going to find a local person to ask." She patted her hand and left.

Aunt Ula let out a short, mirthless laugh. "Turns out that hooker was right."

"What?" Matty hesitated.

Aunt Ula looked at her shoes with a sad smile. "If you make a man feel like a man, he'll die trying to protect you."

The little old woman lifted her head and leaned back against the bench. She stared at the only thing that was familiar on Peach Hill—a sky of purple and gold. The disappearing sun chased a new day to the other side of the world.

Behind her, in the shadows of a drugstore entryway stood a girl in a white dress, leopard-painted hair and cowboy boots. She stood quietly and kept vigil.

Going Home

T he voices of five hundred sopranos and altos filled the auditorium, singing, "help of the helpless, Lord, abide with me." The harmony vibrated in Matty's ears, traveling to her chest. She tried to catch her breath. Her Nana had sung that song in the kitchen—even though she wasn't a church-going woman.

Matty didn't look at Aunt Ula, nor at the other five ladies of Shaded Valley Lutheran. Rows of women sat before and behind her, lining the convention center. Why had she come? She'd dropped by after work on Saturday—to check on the old lady. But why she'd returned for the Sunday morning closing cere-monies didn't make sense.

The women were funny. Even the one who joked about her big Ta-Ta's and kept her wee little dog in her purse. They'd taken Matty into their group, leopard hair and all. No one thought it was strange she'd pretended to be an English woman for Aunt Ula. "Oh, hon," the one named Kay drawled. "I wish I could pull that off. Most of the time she has me *unk*ing like a monkey." Matty had given her a questioning look, but Kay only raised her eyebrows twice and smiled.

The voices swelled. Matty focused on her lap. Her throat clutched, trying to keep a sob throttled. She got up, quickly climbing over the legs of the women, hoping she could get to the lobby.

Still singing, Kay leaned forward, throwing a *Well?* look at Aunt Ula. The old woman held up a finger, sang another verse, and then climbed over legs too.

"I don't know what's the matter with me." Sitting on a bench in the foyer, Matty pushed a tear off her cheek.

"I should've warned you, dear. The music can crack open chinks you've worked hard to seal shut. Happens to all of us. It still catches me by surprise."

"I thought I was fine. We talked. I did my deed and helped you. Why am I crying? What's the matter with me?"

Aunt Ula sat down. "You just met God."

"In there?" Matty hooked a thumb toward the big hall.

"No. The Creator of the Universe has been tapping you on the shoulder between the time you've lived with a grandmother who loved you and the moment you sat down to listen to a cranky old woman on a train. It was the music that finally broke the shell. Now you're draining."

"Why?"

"So you can fill all those empty spaces with something new. Or you can seal yourself back up. Most young do. I did. But take it from me; you'll fill with crap again. And you'll keep cracking. We're crap collectors."

"I don't want to fill up with religious stuff. No offense. But I don't want to become proper or ooze sweetness."

"Well, as Sister Heavé would say, 'Mother Mary and Joseph! Me neither'. Look, you want to know what cracked you open?" Matty nodded. The old woman leaned closer. "You just caught a glimpse of the fact that *you*, beet-juice-wearing Matty, are the cherished property of the Creator of the Universe. You were custom made right down to your leopard-hair and duct-taped boots. You were stolen for a while by your own choices. He bought you back, His esteemed treasure. You're of that much value to the Him."

Matty leaned back against the wall, her boots splayed in front of her as she stared at the ceiling. "If I'm so special, then why don't I do better?"

"Pffffft! And why aren't I Saint Eulalia?" She shook her head. "We're all rebels. We all keep missing the target, and you know what God does? This is the King of Second Chances. He meets you right where you are."

"Why?"

"Love. Unfathomable, ain't it? Those cracks get filled with wisdom, patience, forgiveness, peace...you know...the stuff money can't buy. You may not believe it, but you're different people throughout your life. You'll look back and be mortified at who you were at times. Like crying too much or thinking someone is a coward or saying terrible, hurtful things. Embrace all the toads and saints you've been—because that's you. Your Creator loves you warts and all. Knowing that will help you understand the painful process of being broken and remolded. Your life's a story. It takes many people to help write it."

"Maybe. But if that's so, what's the story with you coming all the way to San Diego to open a time capsule? You waited seventy years to make this trip. You got nothin'!"

"So it would seem." Aunt Ula grinned. "But God pulled a bait-and-switch on me. It seems He gets a hoot out of being crafty. I started with one goal and ended up with something better. I was aching to find proof of my past. Then it dawned on me—what could Kol have possibly put in there that would've lived up to that much anticipation? A note? His hat? Or—and this is what I actually think it was—that damn pipe. I don't remember seeing it after that day. Of course, any of those would've been nice, but I've already been 'cracked' a couple of times learning that "things" don't last. I lost everything we owned when our boat went down. After that, a tornado ran off with the next bunch of stuff I collected." She waved Matty silent. "That's another long story. I think I've finally learned it's best to have treasures that can't be taken away."

"You're just saying stuff to make a crappy situation sound good."

"Oh, sweetie, honestly! When you speak like that, you can expect a good butt-kickin' from wisdom herself. I know what Kol put in there."

Matty's face screwed up in confusion. "What?"

"Love. It was love. Whatever form it was in." A slow smile crossed Aunt Ula's face as she stared at Matty. "This weekend I was given a friend who listened to the scattered pieces of my life, helped me lay them out, end to end. It was like surveying the whole design and seeing my meanderings and leavings made a difference. I went looking for an artifact. I'm going home with healing instead."

The Bay Area Rapid Transit sped by. Through the glass windows of the convention center, the women watched traffic lights turn green. Crowds crossed the street. Others waited.

Singing voices filtered beneath the door of the big hall. Both women sat quietly, listening and watching—Matty sniffling.

"Here. Use the Magic Hankie." The old woman handed her a square of white linen embroidered with yellow flowers. "Keep it. It stops tears."

"I decided last night; I'm going home—to Nana and Texas." Matty dabbed at her eyes.

"Good. It might be hard at first, but you'll sort it out. I finally went home too. Dad was gone. Mom was sick—along with her sister. I took care of those two old women until they died. I think it was what I needed at the time, but didn't know it. It was another healing period, but it sure wasn't easy. Mom never said a word about my eloping. Whenever I brought it up, she waved away the subject. She was dying, so I didn't push it. She didn't want to talk about Joe's bones buried somewhere in Turkey either. It was as though that part of our lives didn't exist. It's strange, those unspoken agreements we make in our families."

"I don't mean to be poking my nose in your business, but I think you need to tell your story to what's left of your family."

Matty twisted her amulet as she talked, making the beet-juice swirl. "It's like living in a dorm room at college. You may decorate it, but it really isn't home. To live there, you have to put out all the pieces that mean something and share them with others. I think if the cracks are really going to heal, you need to tell your story to *them*."

Aunt Ula smiled and looked out at the sky. "God is so sneaky. I thought you were the one getting worked on. I guess it was a two-for-one sale."

Matty giggled. A fresh squirt of tears ran down her cheek. "This hankie isn't working. Is this the one the hooker gave you?"

"It's not the original. That one didn't work either."

"You're a weird old woman."

"Yeah, ain't it great?"

"I hate to leave like this, but I have a lot to do. I'm giving notice at work and heading out the end of this week." She grabbed Aunt Ula and gave her a long hug, whispering in her ear, "I hope you don't run away anymore, but if you hadn't, our lives never would've crossed. Maybe we'll meet again someday."

Aunt Ula nodded. "Maybe."

There was more to say. She wanted to tell her how people would drop into her life for unaccountable reasons, then drop out again. How they tugged and colored the threads of who she was. How loved ones as well as strangers became part of the design. There were so many more lessons—but those would be shared by others. Every part of creation helped with the weaving.

"Thanks for leaving Oklahoma." Matty smiled and waved, her boots clomping on the tiled floor.

Aunt Ula's fingertips barely moved as she watched the young girl walk away.

***

Three of the Lutheran ladies and the tiny dog returned to Oklahoma via Vegas, Boulder Dam, and the Grand Canyon Vera, Kay, and Aunt Ula took the faster route, the train. The conductor traveled up and down the aisle, checking tickets and answering questions. After a while the doors closed, the cars lurched, and the buildings began to slowly pass behind them.

Aunt Ula stared out the window, watching the structures shorten from skyscrapers to three-story offices, and eventually to houses in suburbs. After several miles, the homes became farther apart and finally were replaced by acres of greenery.

Kay leaned next to the old woman. "That was a pretty interesting friend you made. What's her story?"

Aunt Ula gave her a neutral look. "Matty's tale is her own." She returned her gaze to the window, and then hesitated and smiled. "Vera, you may think you're on this train to keep an eye on me, but actually you're here for a story. A chance to listen without being interrupted by a peeing dog or anyone hijacking the conversation. I need for you to hear me." She gave her a stern look. "Really listen, not stare at me like I'm nuts."

"I always pay attention to you." Vera rolled her eyes.

"Tell us," Kay urged.

"Well, this is a story of a sixteen-and-a-half-year-old girl..."

Something fell as she dug in her pocket and pulled out a small metal box. "Mint?" She held up the tin and continued, "For this girl, it started with World War II and her father, a Lutheran pastor, who was born a hundred years old. The only entertainment he allowed was the radio. The only approved suitors were well-scrubbed farmer-boys terrified of his bluster. The young girl didn't pay much attention to the war..."

On the floor, the purple marble had dropped next to her Keds.

It jostled for a while with the sway of the train. At a rough intersection, it rolled across the floor and bounced off Kay's black travel bag. The glass orb hesitated in the aisle a moment, joggling one way, stopping, then slowly jiggling in a lazy circle in the other direction.

The thrum of the train's wheels counted off minutes and miles until at last, the marble meandered away, continuing beneath seats and through lives.

***

Acknowledgements

I'm thankful for all the men and women who left to fight a war (and still do). And I'm overwhelmed by the women who kept the home front strong. They changed women's roles forever.

Thanks to Marina Metevelis, a Rosie the Riveter, and Dr. Josh Smith, Interim Director of the American Merchant Marine, who granted interviews, provided information, and graciously enhanced my knowledge of planes and Mariners.

I appreciate all the folks—strangers and friends—who gladly shared their experiences about WWII and the home front.

Alice Lynn, Ken Knorr, Etta Place, and Orice Klaas, thanks for your technical insights and guidance.

Thanks, to those who fought, worked, died. You remind us that every leaving (in heart or home) is a new beginning.

About the Author

Kris Knorr's droll wit **can also be found in a different genre** described as: stories of stupid cows, wise people, and small-town life written under **Barb Froman.**

She lives in an eye-blink of a town in Oregon with 14 moles and 34 mounds of dirt in the yard.

Here's a path to both of her worlds

Before Morning Breaks: Barb Froman
www.barbfroman.wordpress.com

Lutheran Ladies Circle: Kris Knorr
www.lutheranladies.com

And now...

A sneak peek at a new series...**Coming Soon...**

The Lights of Two Pan

Someone in Two Pan is awake tonight, just like you. Maybe you're standing at the grocery store reading this rather than some rag on how to lose twenty pounds in two weeks. Hopefully, you're lazing in a hammock while the moon rests on long rollers of a warm water ocean. Perhaps you're sitting in a doniker in the Rockies as a single star blazes to its end. God forbid you're trying to rest in some uncomfortable chair or hospital bed waiting—afraid to hope.

Wherever you are, it doesn't matter. Day or night. Or a continent away. Someone in Two Pan is awake with you right now.

It's not a city like New York that never sleeps. It's just that someone in Two Pan isn't sleeping.

In daylight, it's easy to see the residents juggling the uneven pieces of their lives, but come evening, you'd best look for a bit of light to see their struggles. A bare bulb hanging from a tree limb over an open truck hood. The lamp of a bedside vigil, outlining a window. A lantern casting half-shadows across faces in an open field.

In cities, neon bulbs buzz and hum without human company. In Two Pan, a lone point of light means a citizen is making a community improvement, working on her dream, or trying to keep the pieces of his life from crumbling apart.

These are forthright folks. You want an honest opinion, you'll get one. They'll tell you if a casserole needs more seasoning, if you shouldn't have tipped for your last hair cut, or if your nephew is truly dumb and ugly. If you're gullible, they may embellish their advice a bit, but that comes from living in this unyielding land for so long. Sandwiched between granite mountains and tall sky, they've had to create their own diversions.

To find this hidden place, follow Highway 82, a skinny black line on an Eastern Oregon map. Two Pan nestles where it changes into gray patchy asphalt. From there a gut-jostling track takes you into the Eagle Cap Mountains. This little-known path of locals and savvy outdoorsmen winds through the gold camps of yesteryear. Once-exciting places such as Shiny Creek, Lilyville, and French Camp are now trailheads for the semi-daring. Little remains of the gold, in case you were thinking of quitting your job and taking up prospecting.

Local stories are not about the miners, but the folks who stayed to work and prod the land. There must be something in that beggarly soil, because the fifth generation of settlers still owns many of the ranches. And therein lies the great mystery of Two Pan: Why do these folks resist the shift and shuffle of change to stay here?

It's what makes them stubborn, eccentric, and sometimes— a little sleepless.

***

Come visit the folks of Two Pan.

Ebooks and Paperbacks are available through major on-line retailers...or...support your local bookstore and ask to order The Lutheran Ladies *series or the upcoming* Lights of Two Pan *series.*

Thanks for reading!

CPSIA information can be obtained at www.ICGtesting.com
Printed in the USA
LVOW08s0513150514

385679LV00003B/47/P